STUDIES IN ENGLISH LITERATURE

Volume XLIV

SHELLEY'S POLITICAL THOUGHT

by

JOHN POLLARD GUINN

1969
MOUTON
THE HAGUE · PARIS

© Copyright 1969 in The Netherlands.
Mouton & Co. N.V., Publishers, The Hague.

No part of this book may be translated or reproduced in any form by print, photoprint, microfilm, or any other means, without written permission from the publishers.

LIBRARY OF CONGRESS CATALOG CARD NUMBER: 69-17881

Printed in The Netherlands by Mouton & Co., Printers, The Hague.

To *V.L.*

FOREWORD

A concentrated study of any aspect of the works of a major literary figure such as Shelley severely taxes the critical faculties of its author. Not only must he fully employ his own talent, he must also draw from the works of past and contemporary researchers. In this way the body of scholarship grows. Scholars support and complement one another and in a sense stand on each other's shoulders. They frequently manage at the same time to step on each other's toes.

I am appreciative of the many commentators whose works are cited in this study, even those with whom I am not in complete agreement, and I gladly acknowledge my indebtedness to them. I have stood on many shoulders in developing *Shelley's Political Thought*. If I have stepped on some toes, it happened through clumsiness rather than intent.

Special thanks are due Professors M. M. Crow, T. M. Cranfill, and D. L. Miller of the University of Texas for their critical reading of the finished work, and Professor E. E. Stokes of Texas A & M University for permission to use his unpublished thesis, *Shelly and Bernard Shaw: A Study in Late Nineteenth Century Socialism*, as a source. Heartfelt thanks and appreciation go to Professor Willis W. Pratt of the University of Texas for his highly valuable direction and criticism of the work during the period of development. Ultimately it was through the selfless help, encouragement, and sacrifices of my wife, Velma Lee, my son, John, and my daughter, Elizabeth, that the completion of this study became possible. Whatever merit may be found in it is due in large part to the generous help that I have received from family, friends, and colleagues. The deficiencies are entirely my own.

Austin, Texas J.P.G.
October 4, 1968

TABLE OF CONTENTS

Foreword 7
I. The Growth of Shelley's Early Political Thought . 11
II. Early Objectives of Political Reform 27
III. Political Tracts after 1815 45
IV. Political Thought in Poetry after 1815 68
V. Shelley's Political Influence 96
Bibliography 132

I

THE GROWTH OF SHELLEY'S EARLY POLITICAL THOUGHT

Scholarship has demolished the myths that almost inevitably sprang from the unorthodox life and thought of Shelley, so that we now have a reasonably clear picture of his life and sound interpretations of his works. The total output of the scholars gives us an insight that was beyond the range of possibility for our predecessors, but many an unsolved problem remains. A very important one concerns Shelley's political philosophy, the topic of this study. Though it has been partially explored, a full survey has not appeared. My task of collecting, defining, analyzing, and tracing the influence of Shelley's political doctrine is rendered all the more pleasant and absorbing because of the labor of my predecessors.

Shelley is famous as a poet. His best poetry reflects the highest standards of art. Beautiful language and highly original imagery shadow forth human truths. There is no didacticism in it. Yet an impulse to move men toward reform of their lives and social institutions is his constant and deepest source of inspiration. Though much concerned with establishing a name for himself as a poet, he would have preferred to be remembered as a reformer. Evidence of this is discernible in almost every phase of his life and works. His youthful effort to bring about reform in Ireland in 1812 and succeeding attempts to remedy grievances of the English tell us that he considered politics the starting point for reform. Many of his important poems embody political views, and his prose works provide extensive discussions of political principles.

The goal toward which Shelley's thought on politics was

directed was the production of human happiness. Theory that could not be applied to this end had no value for him. It is therefore not surprising that he undertook projects in Ireland and England similar to those of Tom Paine in America and France.

Like Paine, whom he admired, Shelley was both a political theorist and missionary. He was, in a sense, a politician. Though he never held or sought public office, he was brought up in the expectation that he would succeed his father as a member of Parliament.[1] He tried to acquaint people with ideas that would enable them to voice their grievances and thus establish a body of enlightened public opinion which authorities would not dare ignore. Gaining redress of grievances and reform of political institutions as a result of the weight of public opinion is a fundamental principle of democracy, and Shelley did not underestimate its value in a day when the wealthy and aristocratic governing classes were contemptuous of all that did not serve their own interests. He saw more clearly, perhaps, than any of his contemporaries the futility of violence as a means of securing reform. Unlike Paine, he had no selfish interest in the publication of his political views and never undertook the promotion of political ideas with a view toward personal gain.

Since the principles which would further the welfare and happiness of all people are of necessity those moral principles which should govern relationships between individuals, a government seeking to promote this goal would make them its basic laws. This was Shelley's doctrine. An insistence upon the identity of fundamental political and moral principles tends to give his political philosophy its utopian hue.[2] His proposals for specific

---

[1] Shortly before his expulsion from Oxford, Shelley wrote a letter, dated March 2, 1811, to Leigh Hunt, editor of *The Examiner*, in which he says, "My father is in parliament, and on attaining twenty-one, I shall in all probability fill his vacant seat." For the full text of this letter, which reflects Shelley's keen interest in, and knowledge of, politics, see *The Complete Works of Percy Bysshe Shelley*, edited by Roger Ingpen and Walter E. Peck, Julian Editions, vol. VIII, pp. 55-56 (this work is hereinafter referred to as *Julian Works*).

[2] In a letter of January 7, 1812, to Elizabeth Hitchener, Shelley says, "Southey says Expedience ought to [be] made the ground of politics but not of morals. I urged that the most fatal error that ever happened in the world

reforms, however, reveal a knowledge of political realities which is at odds with utopianism. Some reform was always better than none. Large reforms could be accomplished only in small, slow steps. He would do the expedient thing to secure an objective, provided that it did not entail violence. With this concept of Shelley as a political thinker and reformer in view, we may now examine his origins and growth – particularly his family's connections and interests, and the early manifestations of his political ideals as they are revealed in his activities, letters, essays and prose tracts, and poetry.[3]

If we seek the beginning of Shelley's political thought, we must view, however sketchily, the history of the political interests of the Shelley family. Shelley's grandfather, Sir Bysshe, though not primarily a politician, was to some extent involved in politics.[4] Newman Ivey White writes of him,

He was ... [in 1790] one of the wealthiest landholders in ... [Sussex]. The Duke of Norfolk, one of the Whig leaders who possessed considerable holdings in the district, became alive to his possibilities of political usefulness. Such a man as Bysshe, no doubt, was also alert to the advantages of benefiting from the Duke's interests. In 1806, therefore, Mr. Bysshe Shelley was made a baronet, apparently in anticipation of services still to be performed for the Whigs.

Thus Sir Bysshe brilliantly accomplished rather more than his early

---

was the separation of political and ethical science" (*Julian Works*, vol. VIII, p. 235).

Again in *A Philosophical View of Reform*, written in 1819-1820 but not published until 1920, Shelley says, "Morals and politics can only be considered as portions of the same science" (*Shelley's Prose*, edited by David Lee Clark, p. 253) (this work is hereinafter referred to as *Shelley's Prose*).

[3] Kenneth Neill Cameron's *The Young Shelley* and Carl Grabo's *The Magic Plant* are especially serviceable as guides to the early phase of Shelley's politics, and Newman Ivey White's biography (*Shelley*, two volumes) is indispensable to any branch of Shelley research. Therefore, these works, in addition to the most useful editions of Shelley – notably *Shelley's Prose*, the Oxford and Cambridge editions of the poetry, and volumes VIII, IX, and X of the *Julian Works*, which contain the letters – will be the principal sources in the study of the beginnings of Shelley's political philosophy.

[4] See Newman Ivey White's *Shelley*, vol. I, pp. 3-11, for an account of Shelley's ancestry, with particular attention to the attainments of Sir Bysshe. Kenneth Neill Cameron's *The Young Shelley*, pp. 37-39, also gives a glimpse of Sir Bysshe's political connections and activities.

ambition to found a house. He had raised his own branch of the Shelley family from an obscure, modestly endowed line of country gentlemen to a wealthy family with a baronetcy.[5]

The Duke of Norfolk was a liberal, or Foxite, Whig. The Whig Party during this period, though serving as the opposition to the Tories, who were in power, was made up of several factions, some of whom were landed gentry with views similar to those of the Tories. The liberals in the Whig Party were led by Charles Fox. This group advocated governmental reforms and sympathized with the revolutionists in France. They were looked upon with disfavor and distaste by many Whigs as well as Tories. The Duke of Norfolk, the mentor of our Shelley family in a political sense, was one of only six peers who supported Fox.[6]

Sir Bysshe and the Duke of Norfolk were undoubtedly drawn together politically by economic considerations. Both were wealthy sheep raisers and could, by joining forces with other sheep raisers, fight for governmental protection against the flooding of England's woolen markets with imported wool and the encroachments of the newly developed cotton industry. But an identity of economic interests is probably not the whole story of Sir Bysshe's alliance with Norfolk. He was born in America and acquired eminence as a result of his own enterprise and a fortunate second marriage. Such a background would tend to place his sympathies with liberals rather than conservatives. Kenneth Neill Cameron says, "even to the end of his life ... he exhibited strange 'democratic' ways".[7]

Sir Bysshe's political connection with the Duke of Norfolk resulted in his son Timothy's election to the House of Commons in 1790 as a Whig. He was elected for the Horsham borough, but irregularities which provided his opponents grounds for contesting the election unseated him. Shortly afterward, however, he was elected member of Parliament for New Shoreham at the instiga-

---

[5] N. I. White, *Shelley*, vol. I, p. 9.
[6] The three basic policies of the Foxite liberals were, "reform of Parliament (by abolishing rotten boroughs and extending the franchise); Catholic emancipation (aimed mainly at alleviating the subjugation of Ireland); and peace with France" (K. N. Cameron, *The Young Shelley*, p. 43).
[7] K. N. Cameron, *The Young Shelley*, p. 38.

tion of the Duke, and this event marked the beginning of his long political career in office. His record seems to fully justify White's observation that "During his long service in Parliament he was entirely undistinguished".[8] White adds, "[Timothy] seemed content to limit his services by voting consistently as the Whig interests of the Duke of Norfolk required." [9] We find, however, that Sir Timothy [10] became a conservative Whig in his later years. In 1835 he opposed the reform candidate Robert Henry Hurst. This was his last appearance as an office seeker.[11] If his growing conservatism clashed in any palpable way with Norfolk's liberalism, the fact has escaped the notice of commentators.

Regarding the politics of Sussex, the county in which the Shelley family flourished, Cameron concedes that traditionally it may have been what White said it was, "the most conservative county in England",[12] but he then shows from Parliamentary records that it was the center of reform activities during a period that encompasses Shelley's life.[13] Though no evidence has been uncovered showing that Shelley came in contact with local reformers, there is a possibility that he did. If so, he may very well have been influenced by them.

The youthful Shelley was certainly no stranger to his grandfather, Sir Bysshe, who "allowed his son Timothy the use of Field Place [one of his estates and the birthplace of Shelley] but disliked him heartily and used to curse him, even in the presence

[8] White, *op. cit.*, vol. I, p. 12.
[9] *Ibid.*
[10] Timothy became Sir Timothy in 1815 upon the death of Sir Bysshe.
[11] See Cameron, *op. cit.*, p. 40.
[12] White, *op. cit.*, vol. I, p. 15.
[13] Cameron, *op. cit.*, p. 40, says, "certainly Horsham had a goodly bloc of progressive votes; Hurst [a liberal] was elected at least twice, and the whole county [of Sussex] was a center of reform agitation in the 1830's. In 1814, Horsham petitioned Parliament to abolish the slave trade." Quoting *Parliamentary Debates, published under the superintendence of T. C. Hansard*, he continues, "in 1817, 'a large reform meeting was held in front of the "Lamb Inn"', the magistrates having refused permission to hold it in the Town Hall because the notice for the meeting did not restrict it to property owners but invited 'all labourers, mechanics, and apprentices'. The Meeting was considered sufficiently important to warrant comment in the House of Commons and Sir Timothy arose to testify to its orderliness."

of young Percy Bysshe, his grandson".[14] After a careful examination of the evidence concerning the personalities of those members of Shelley's family with whom Shelley associated during his childhood, White concludes, concerning Shelley's early political proclivities,

> these traits [unconventionality of dress, religious opinion, conduct, etc.] are distinctly sporadic rather than characteristic [of Shelley's relatives], and it might be maintained that they are no more than accidental. If one must look for an exterior explanation of the poet's character one will find it more in the times than in any discernible heredity or environment.[15]

Cameron, on the other hand, presents a convincing argument that Shelley was influenced in his early political thought and activity to a much greater extent than White supposed by his immediate environment – if the word "environment" may be used to include the talk and activity of friends and relatives as well as general circumstances. In the first place, he draws the following conclusions regarding the effect upon Shelley of Sir Bysshe's political connections with such a Whig as the Duke of Norfolk and of Sir Timothy's subsequent election to Parliament:

> the Whig connections of the Shelley family ... mean, for one thing, that Shelley from an early age lived and breathed a political atmosphere. In most English upper-class families, politics is a major subject of discussion; in a family, the father of which is a Member of Parliament, it is likely to become a daily diet. Sir Timothy, even though not distinguished for his volubility in Parliament – a search through *Hansard* reveals only the brief speech on the Horsham reform meeting – was nevertheless a loyal party man and doubtless discussed the daily events of the House and the issues of the day in the bosom of his family; and the young Percy probably also got liberal doses of Whigism from Sir Bysshe and the Duke of Norfolk (whose nearby estate he visited).[16]

The second element of Cameron's argument is that Shelley's early life was directed toward a professional political career. There is ample biographical evidence to support such a contention. For example, the statement in Shelley's letter of March 2, 1811, to Leigh Hunt, alluded to earlier, that "My father is in parliament,

[14] White, *op. cit.*, vol. I, p. 10.
[15] *Ibid.*, vol. I, p. 15.
[16] Cameron, *op. cit.*, pp. 40-41.

and on attaining twenty-one I shall in all probability fill his vacant seat",[17] is a considered expression of expectations and reveals that the Shelley family looked upon Percy as Sir Timothy's political heir. It reveals also that Shelley himself, despite youthful uncertainty and desire to mold his own life, had acquiesced in his family's plans.

In the third place, Thomas Jefferson Hogg's emphasis in his Shelley biography upon Shelley's dislike of politics and politicians is wrong. His presentation of Shelley's March 2, 1811, letter to Hunt reveals this. The account of Shelley's career at Oxford (October, 1810-March, 1811) does not mention it. The letter appears, however, with correspondence of the 1812-1813 period, when Shelley was at Tanyrallt, Wales. Insertion of the letter among the related matters of Shelley's Oxford days would have discredited Hogg's story of Shelley's dislike for politics. But the story is falsified by Hogg himself when he attempts to disguise the letter's significance. He says that Shelley's failure to tell him about it during their days at Oxford indicates that Shelley was ashamed of having written it.[18]

Finally, it is possible to show that the political issues of the time of Shelley's childhood and youth, and the Foxite Whigs' stand on them, are at the core of Shelley's first political expressions and activities. Cameron writes,

> Those who are acquainted with Shelley's political thinking will see many of the germs of it in these Whig doctrines: ... the sympathy for the French and American Revolutions; the advocacy of the extension of the franchise; the championing of the Irish; the preference of brief "anarchy" to prolonged "despotism"; the faith that the "mighty changes of the rising world", will overthrow "the monuments of tyranny and injustice", and move on to "a happy and glorious consummation".[19]

Consequently, Shelley's extensive political inheritance, an aspect of his life that has not been sufficiently emphasized by biographers, coupled with the momentous political events of his early

---

[17] *Julian Works*, vol. VIII, p. 56.
[18] See Thomas Jefferson Hogg, *The Life of Percy Bysshe Shelley* (1906 edition), p. 380.
[19] Cameron, *op. cit.*, p. 45.

years, largely accounts for his interest in political reform from almost the beginning of his writing career.

"The Irishman's Song" (October, 1809), tenth poem of *Original Poetry by Victor and Cazire*, one of Shelley's first published works, has as its theme the unjust treatment which Ireland was receiving at the hands of England and the undying resolution of the Irish people to gain revenge.[20] It provides evidence that the thought of the seventeen-year-old Shelley ran at least partly in political lines. A survey of his early publications shows a rapid and complete change from a preoccupation with Gothic horror to political reform.

Further evidence of the early growth of Shelley's interest in political affairs is a letter written to a newspaper in support of Grenville's candidacy for the office of Chancellor of Oxford. The letter appeared in the November 15, 1809, issue of *The Morning Chronicle* and, according to Thomas Medwin, was signed "A Master of Arts of Oxford".[21] Grenville, a right-wing Whig, favored Catholic emancipation. This was the only issue on which he and the Foxite reformers agreed. His stand on this question no doubt enabled Shelley to endorse him and serves to emphasize the fact that Shelley was, even at an early age, the practical politician when occasion demanded.

Politics was not only a common subject of conversation in Shelley's boyhood home but a congenial one. White observes,

At Field Place in the summer of 1810 there was much dinner talk on

---

[20] Cameron believes that "The Irishman's Song" reflects Whig influence upon Shelley's early political thought. He says (*op. cit.*, p. 46), "In view of the Foxite Whigs' position on the Irish question and the Duke of Norfolk's consistent championing of Catholic emancipation, we need infer no other than Whig influence to account for this poem."

[21] The account of the authorship of the letter, though involved, establishes beyond reasonable doubt that Shelley had a hand in writing it. White says (*op. cit.*, vol. I, Note #14 of Chapter V, p. 586) that Dennis Florence MacCarthy (*Shelley's Early Life* (1872), p. 24), who found the letter in *The Morning Chronicle* which Thomas Medwin (*Revised Life of Shelley*, ed. H. B. Forman (1913), pp. 86-87) asserts that Shelley wrote, "thinks [the letter] was written in part for his father". Shelley's father, White observes (*op. cit.*, vol. I, p. 75), was "Master of Arts of University College [Oxford]" and favored Catholic emancipation, as did the Duke of Norfolk.

politics, Sir Francis Burdett, and the state of the nation – talk that seems to have been entirely to Bysshe's taste.[22]

Lines from a poem by Elizabeth Shelley in *Original Poetry* mention the political discussions:

> Then to politics turn, of Burdett's reformation,
> One declares it would hurt, t'other better the nation,
> Will ministers keep? sure they've acted quite wrong,
> The burden this is of each morning-call song.[23]

The Burdett referred to in these lines is Sir Francis, an advocate of reform around whom the liberal element of the Whig party rallied. Shelley's admiration for, and endorsement of, Burdett's political activities is evinced in the dedication of *The Wandering Jew*, Shelley's first long poem. This work, published in Edinburgh in the summer of 1810, Shelley dedicated to Burdett in glowing terms:

> To Sir Francis Burdett, bart., M. P., in consideration of the active virtues by which both his public and private life is so eminently distinguished, the following poem is inscribed by the author.[24]

As Cameron points out, the significance of this dedication is that it occurred shortly after Burdett had been imprisoned in the Tower upon incurring the displeasure of the House of Commons when he made a scathing attack upon it for sending one John Gale Jones to prison. He had denounced its decision to hold in secret an inquiry into the disastrous Walcheren expedition against the French.[25]

It is clear enough that Shelley did not compose *The Wandering Jew* with a view toward dedicating it to Sir Francis Burdett. The decision to dedicate the poem to Sir Francis was made at the last moment before the poem was published, and it would seem that the poem, endowed with many of the trappings of the Gothic

---

[22] White, *op. cit.*, vol. I, p. 75.
[23] Lines 9-12 of the second poem, dated April 30, 1810, of *Original Poetry by Victor and Cazire* as they appear in *The Complete Poetical Works of Percy Bysshe Shelley*, edited by Thomas Hutchinson (Oxford University Press, 1933), p. 844 (this work is hereinafter referred to as *Oxford Works*).
[24] *Julian Works*, vol. IV, p. 349.
[25] See Cameron, *op. cit.*, pp. 48-49.

tale of horror, is to say the least an unusual tribute to courageous action for the sake of political principles. It is a youthful practice work and has little to recommend it as literature. Its plot derives from the fragment of a translation of Schubart's German poem, *The Wandering Jew*, and owes something to the figure of the Wandering Jew in M. G. Lewis' *The Monk*. The fragmentary translation of Schubart's poem, with the exception of the final sentence, which indicates that the Almighty Tyrant was appeased, Shelley later published in *Notes to Queen Mab*. The Wandering Jew was to appear as a symbolic figure with changed meaning from time to time in later works of Shelley.[26] White says, "Shelley's first Wandering Jew is a rather orthodox creation ... and is thus a witness to the fact that Shelley's religious opinions were still largely orthodox." [27] Yet Shelley's dedication of "a rather orthodox" Wandering Jew to a political rebel is prophetic, for the character soon came to symbolize Shelley's own rebellious hatred of the "Almighty Tyrant", author of the hero's suffering. This is apparent in "The Wandering Jew's Soliloquy", a poem which Shelley wrote "probably about the time ... [that he] began *Queen Mab*",[28] i.e., in 1812. Here Ahasuerus, the Wandering Jew, addresses the Author of his suffering thus:

> Tyrant of Earth! pale misery's jackal thou!
> Are there no stores of vengeful violent fate
> Within the magazines of thy fierce hate?
> . . . .
> Yes! I would court a ruin such as this,
> Almighty Tyrant! and give thanks to Thee –
> Drink deeply – drain the cup of hate –
>   remit this I may die.[29]

Hence the dedication of *The Wandering Jew* to a man who demonstrated that he had the courage of his political convictions,

---

[26] An excellent summary of the evolution of the Wandering Jew in Shelley's thought is provided by White, *op. cit.*, vol. I, Note #14 of Chapter XI, p. 653.
[27] White, *op. cit.*, vol. I, p. 60.
[28] *Ibid.*, vol. I, Note #14 of Chapter XI, p. 653.
[29] Lines 11-13 and 27-29 of "The Wandering Jew's Soliloquy", *The Complete Poetical Works of Percy Bysshe Shelley* (Student's Cambridge Edition, 1901), p. 573 (this work is hereinafter referred to as *Cambridge Works*).

THE GROWTH OF SHELLEY'S EARLY POLITICAL THOUGHT   21

by Shelley, to whom the Wandering Jew ultimately symbolized defiance of tyranny, points to Shelley's intention to fight tyranny wherever it might be found, in whatever form, with special attention to political tyranny.[30]

After the dedication of *The Wandering Jew* to Burdett, Shelley's active interest in politics becomes increasingly evident. Shelley biographers inform us that his political principles at this time were becoming republican. White, quoting Thomas Jefferson Hogg, presents some evidence concerning Shelley's republicanism in 1811 during the latter part of his brief stay at Oxford:

In the matter of politics, "Shelley was entirely devoted to the lovely theory of freedom; but he was also eminently averse at that time from engaging in the far less beautiful practices wherein are found the actual and operative energies of liberty". "His feelings and behaviour were in many respects highly aristocratic" and his fastidious spirit was offended by many of the crudenesses of democracy, even while he was "wholly republican" in theory.[31]

White believes that Hogg's impression of Shelley's "aristocratic" manner is substantiated to some extent by the comments of others who knew Shelley and by Shelley's own statements. He observes,

This same streak of aristocratic prejudice seems indicated by Shelley, Mary, and Jane Clairmont in occasional references in their journals of 1814 to their fellow travellers down the Rhine and again in Shelley's treatment of the "swinish multitude" in *Swellfoot the Tyrant*, in 1820. Stockdale [one of Shelley's publishers] hints an impression similar to Hogg's.[32]

Any contradiction between Shelley's manner and his professed democratic principles must have been superficial. A word about his life and the meaning of "democracy" will show this. In the

---

[30] Cameron, *op. cit.*, p. 49, sees Shelley's dedication of *The Wandering Jew* to Burdett as a move by Shelley to cast in his lot with the political reformers for whom *Cobbett's Political Register* and Hunt's *Examiner* were spokesmen. It was a reprinting of Burdett's speech in *Cobbett's Political Register* that brought down the wrath of Parliament upon Burdett and resulted in his being sent to the Tower. John and Leigh Hunt supported Burdett against both the Tories and many members of the Whig party as well.
[31] White, *op. cit.*, vol. I, p. 107.
[32] *Ibid.*, vol. I, pp. 596-597.

first place, Shelley was reared in a home that maintained relatively high standards of taste, and no one who knew him ever failed to be aware of his unusual intellectual powers and keen sensitiveness. He was a highly intelligent, sensitive, well-bred person. The words "democratic" and "republican" do not imply a repudiation of the canons of taste. On the contrary, they imply the aim of elevating the standard of taste of the masses and of sharpening their intellectual faculties. It is difficult to see, therefore, that Shelley's disapproval of inferior thought or deed contradicts his democratic principles. If democracy does not mean the adoption of the lowest standards of human behavior by all members of society, neither does it mean the abolition of the privilege of choosing one's friends. It does not impose uniformity of thought and choice. Put in the simplest terms it means that one must reserve for every other member of society the same right to think and act that he reserves for himself. This enables one to choose and judge for himself without being snobbish. In the second place, a multitude of people, or mob, may very well perform "swinish" deeds, even though no individual member would be likely to degrade himself by performing the same deeds alone. Mob action debases all members of the mob by arousing their worst passions and cloaking them in anonymity. Disapproval of anything that smacks of mob action, therefore, does not of necessity imply an aristocratic attitude. Finally, Shelley's willingness to help others, regardless of their station in life, is evidence of a nature that could hardly be described as haughty.

Another evidence of Shelley's early political views exists in *The Posthumous Fragments of Margaret Nicholson*, a small volume of poetry which Shelley composed in October and November of 1810 and which was published by November 17, 1810.[33] The volume, as the title indicates, was attributed to Margaret Nicholson, "a mad washerwoman ... who had attempted to assassinate George III, twenty-five years before",[34] and was still living at the

---

[33] White's Note #51 of Chapter V, *op. cit.*, vol. I, p. 590, reads: "*Posthumous Fragments of Margaret Nicholson* was advertised in the *Oxford Herald* of November 17 [1810] as 'just published'."

[34] White, *op. cit.*, vol. I, pp. 92-93.

time of publication. Shelley's name was not associated with the work, and Hogg claims that at his suggestion Shelley published it as a burlesque: "[the poems of *Posthumous Fragments*] were edited by 'John Fitz-Victor', who was described as ... Margaret Nicholson's nephew. It added to the joke that Fitz-Victor meant also to the initiate 'son of Victor', co-author of *Original Poetry by Victor and Cazire*." [35] Shelley commentators, however, are in agreement with White's judgment that the poems were not written as a prank: "It seems very doubtful that the poems were deliberately burlesqued in the manner described by Hogg. They read no more like burlesque than Shelley's previous poetry." [36] In fact the two most important poems of the six in the volume – the two that bear political implications – "War" and "Epithalamium of Francis Ravaillac and Charlotte Corday", are "revolutionary attacks upon despotism".[37]

"War", the first and most important poem of the *Margaret Nicholson* volume, reveals that Shelley's hatred of the monarchical system of government had become fixed by the time he entered Oxford in October, 1810, at the age of eighteen. Its theme is that monarchy causes war, society's worst affliction; abolition of monarchy will result in peace.[38] Cameron sees in the poem an implied advocacy of a full-blown republican form of government.[39] Though it is hardly possible to see this without having some preconceived ideas, it is clear that one who writes seriously upon the theme entertains little enthusiasm for any form of monarchical government.

The dedication of *The Wandering Jew* to Burdett and the composition of the *Margaret Nicholson* poems that have political impact occur during the period in Shelley's life when he was discarding the possibility of accepting the social and political doctrines of established institutions and adopting only those that withstood the test of his own experience and observation. It must

[35] *Ibid.*, vol. I, p. 93. White's remarks are based upon Hogg's account.
[36] *Ibid.*, vol. I, p. 93.
[37] *Ibid.*
[38] Parts of "Epithalamium of Francis Ravaillac and Charlotte Corday" express the same idea.
[39] Cameron, *op. cit.*, p. 55.

be said, it seems to me, that Shelley was discarding the possibility of accepting established social and political doctrines rather than discarding the doctrines themselves, for there is no evidence that he ever really accepted them.

According to Hogg, Shelley became a republican during his Oxford days (October, 1810-March, 1811). Some of his activities support this contention. On March 2, 1811, he wrote a letter introducing himself to Leigh Hunt, editor of *The Examiner* (see above, p. 12. Footnote # 1). In it he congratulates Hunt upon being acquitted of charges brought against him because he criticized the army for having soldiers flogged, proposes a course of action for strengthening the liberal faction in the government, expresses the expectation that he himself will succeed his father in Parliament when he comes of age, and expresses the hope that future circumstances will enable him to devote all of his effort to advancing the cause of liberty.[40] It is an effort to align himself with Hunt and the liberals for whom he was a spokesman. His aim of forming a society which would be strong enough to voice opposition to governmental policies suggests the kind of enterprise he was soon to attempt in Ireland.[41]

Shelley's growing republican feelings may be associated with the Finnerty case. In his support of the movement to aid Peter Finnerty, "an Irish journalist who had ... been sentenced to eighteen months' imprisonment for speaking his mind to Lord Castlereagh in a letter published in the *Morning Chronicle*",[42] Cameron finds evidence of his change from the principles of the Whig party to those of republicanism.[43] Burdett, Leigh Hunt, and other liberals came to Finnerty's defense. Shelley contributed a guinea to the cause. In addition he "caused to be advertised in ... [*The Oxford University and City Herald*] for March 8 [1811], 'A Poetical Essay on the Existing State of Things, By a Gentleman of the University of Oxford, for assisting to maintain in

[40] For the text of the letter, see *Julian Works*, vol. VIII, pp. 55-56.
[41] Cameron observes, *op. cit.*, p. 53, "A year or so later ... just such an organization as Shelley here advocates did originate in the Hampden Clubs."
[42] The quoted words are White's (*op. cit.*, vol. I, pp. 107-108).
[43] See Cameron, *op. cit.*, pp. 49-50.

Prison Mr. Peter Finnerty, imprisoned for libel' ".[44] The poem, if it was ever written, has not been found, but participation in the Finnerty case shows that he was beginning to oppose actively the tyranny of the English monarchy.

The story of Shelley's childhood and schoolboy days, it would seem, is the story of a search for basic social and political principles which if acted upon would yield happiness and contentment for human beings in the here and now. At some time during his later Eton days, or at Oxford, he began to find some of the answers he had been seeking, because during this period he became acquainted with Godwin's *Political Justice*, a work that had profound influence upon his political thinking. Here was a work that provided a rational foundation for conclusions that he had grasped as the result of unhappy personal experience with many of his teachers and fellows at Eton and Oxford as well as with members of his family. As his intellectual horizons expanded, he observed that the causes of his own anguish were at work in the world on an infinitely larger scale. Shelley had discovered at this early period of his life that tyranny is a personal matter, whatever its form, and that human beings, whatever else they may be, must be free. Hence, *Political Justice* appeared to him to be a handbook of instructions for the production of human freedom, because it was a rational analysis of conditions under which freedom would be possible. His enthusiasm for the work is reflected in his letter to Godwin, dated January 10, 1812:

[*Political Justice*] opened to my mind fresh and more extensive views; it materially influenced my character, and I rose from its perusal a wiser and a better man. I was no longer the votary of romance; till then I had existed in an ideal world – now I found that in this universe of ours was enough to excite the interest of the heart, enough to employ the discussions of reason; I beheld, in short, that I had duties to perform.[45]

It is common knowledge that Shelley draws heavily upon *Political Justice* in his later writings. However, there is reason to suspect that he is overstating the case when he asserts that before reading

---

[44] White, *op. cit.*, vol. I, p. 108.
[45] *Julian Works*, vol. VIII, p. 240.

it he "had existed in an ideal world", for politics were an important part of his family environment. *Political Justice* may very well have moved Shelley to formulate a political doctrine and to act upon it, but political ideas were hardly new to him when he first read the book. Be that as it may, by March, 1811, the time of his expulsion from Oxford, Shelley had begun an independent life as a reformer, and political reform was his first order of business.

II

EARLY OBJECTIVES OF POLITICAL REFORM

Shelley's political ideals are sometimes stated and acclaimed in his poetry. More often they are symbolized in this genre. They are, however, fully developed and commented upon in certain of his prose works. Before 1815 Shelley produced five such works: *An Address to the Irish People, Proposals for an Association of Philanthropists, A Declaration of Rights, A Letter to Lord Ellenborough,* and *On the Punishment of Death.* Of these the first two are the most important.

The measure of the importance of these works is to be found in what they reveal of the growth of Shelley's political ideas rather than in their influence or inherent value. Like other anonymous tracts of the time, they would have remained in limbo had Shelley's posthumous fame not attracted attention to them. By the end of the Irish venture Shelley himself knew that he could not accomplish the objectives of his political tracts:

I shall address myself no more to the illiterate. I will look to events in which it will be impossible that I can share, and make myself the cause of an effect which will take place ages after I have mouldered in the dust. ... Wholly to abstract our views from self, undoubtedly requires unparalleled disinterestedness. There is not a completer abstraction than labouring for distant ages.[1]

In view of the importance that Shelley has attained since death, it would almost seem as though he foresaw everything. His certainty that those principles which he championed without success would eventually take hold is a significant part of his political thought. His observations concerning failure to hasten

[1] Shelley to Godwin, March 18, 1812, *Julian Works,* vol. VIII, p. 301.

political reform in Ireland could apply with equal truth and force to his other attempts at reform:

> I had done all that I could do; if its effects were beneficial, they were not greatly so. I am dissatisfied with my success, but not with the attempt.[2]

The elements constituting the Irish problem which Shelley undertook to solve were deep-rooted and infinitely complicated. During the last thirty years of the eighteenth century the complex struggle of the Irish against their English oppressors began to revive after a long period of quiescence. At first the initiative was taken by the Irish Protestants, who controlled the whole of Ireland, because they resented the fact that Ireland was sacrificed to English trading interests and that only members of the Anglican church were accorded political privileges, though most of the population were either Roman Catholics or non-Anglican Protestants. During the American Revolutionary War Irish volunteers, who were Protestants, got ready to defend against French invasion of Ireland, but their terms for doing this were the removal of commercial disabilities and the complete separation of the Irish Parliament from control by the British. They gained free markets, but Catholics were still allowed no part in the Dublin government. The rotten boroughs were controlled in such a way as to necessitate a reform bill before even the Protestants could become self-governing.

Hence Protestants and Catholics in Ireland, both at the mercy of their English masters, came to tolerate each other during the eighteenth century; but with the anti-Jacobin feeling combined with the no-Popery cry that went up in England, it became apparent that Irish help against France could not be procured by the British. The French offer of liberty to Ireland set Irish Protestants against Catholics again. They found themselves once more fighting the battles of the English in helping to crush the rebellion of 1798.

By 1801 Pitt decided that union was the only method of restoring order and justice, but he did not have enough power to

[2] Shelley to Elizabeth Hitchener, *ca.* April 16, 1812, *ibid.*, vol. VIII, p. 308.

emancipate Roman Catholics, a measure which he had formulated as a means of bribing the majority of the Irish people into acceptance of the Act of Union. However, the mere promise of political emancipation, coupled with the corruption of the Parliament at Dublin, was sufficient to secure passage.

The savage struggle in Ireland went forward amid race hatred, religious antagonism, and economic exploitation by means of absentee-landlordism and rack rent. The masses were granted no educational opportunities. Union with England in 1801 brought no real improvements. Catholic disabilities had not been removed by 1812, the date of Shelley's arrival. Conditions such as these, the accumulation of generations of Irish degradation and bitterness, were viewed with cynicism by such a would-be political reformer as Godwin, who did his utmost to dissuade Shelley from the Irish venture. Shelley, however, at nineteen, already having been expelled from Oxford, estranged from his family, and married to a girl who was little more than a child, did not lack the youthful enthusiasm and energy to attack in person the world's most complex contemporary political problem.

The *Address* is the beginning of Shelley's attempt to help the Irish achieve the political reform that they desperately needed. His motive for writing it appears in the first sentence: "Fellowmen, I am not an Irishman, yet I can feel for you." [3] He had, in fact, the capacity of putting himself in the place of others to an astonishing degree. As a result he could see clearly not only the basic causes of political maneuvers but the effects of political power upon both those who wielded it and those upon whom it was brought to bear. It has been said, with some justification, that he lacked the instinct of self-preservation. However that may be, it was his sympathy for the downtrodden that led him to write the *Address* and undertake the whole Irish venture. The work was intended for "the poor Irish Catholics" and aimed at bestowing upon "uneducated apprehensions ideas of liberty, benevolence, peace, and toleration".[4] Secretly it was to serve as

[3] *Shelley's Prose*, p. 40.
[4] Shelley to Elizabeth Hitchener, January 20, 1812, *Julian Works*, vol. VIII, p. 246 and Shelley to Elizabeth Hitchener, January 26, 1812, *ibid.*, vol. VIII, p. 254.

"a preliminary to other pamphlets to shake Catholicism at its basis, and induce Quakerish and Socinian principles of politics, without objecting to the Christian religion".[5]

The *Address* to the Irish Catholics presents arguments designed to fulfill these expressed intentions. The question of Catholic emancipation involves the problem of the relationship between religion and politics. An examination of the history of both Roman Catholicism and Protestantism leads to the conclusion that there is nothing in either religion to warrant the exclusive possession of political power by its advocates, for each sect in turn had been guilty of persecuting the other when invested with governmental authority. Shelley perceives that oppression in the name of religion and race really stems from human greed:

> There are many Englishmen who cry down the Irish and think it answers their ends to revile all that belongs to Ireland; but it is not because these men are Englishmen that they maintain such opinions, but because they wish to get money, and titles, and power. They would act in this manner to whatever country they might belong, until mankind is much altered for the better, which reform, I hope, will one day be effected.[6]

Shelley's secret purpose of calling into question the motives of the quest for political power by Roman Catholicism appears when he warns that Catholic emancipation alone will only replace one tyranny with another:

> Some teach you that others are heretics, that you alone are right; some teach that rectitude consists in religious opinions, without which no morality is good. Some will tell you that you ought to divulge your secrets to one particular set of men. Beware, my friends, how you trust those who speak in this way. They will, I doubt not, attempt to rescue you from your present miserable state, but they will prepare a worse.[7]

The plea for Catholic emancipation is in effect a plea for religious freedom and a separation of church and state. This is made clear by the advocacy of a moral foundation for political institutions.

---

[5] Shelley to Elizabeth Hitchener, January 26, 1812, *ibid.*, vol. VIII, p. 254.
[6] *Shelley's Prose*, pp. 40-41.
[7] *Ibid.*, p. 41.

The moral virtues of honesty, justice (fair play), and the wisdom of reason exist apart from religious belief, Shelley argues. He concludes, therefore, that "there is no reason . . . why every religion, every form of thinking might not be tolerated".[8] People, however, must seek a system of government under which they can be free rather than one which merely tolerates, because toleration is not the opposite, but the counterfeit, of intolerance. Hence he writes, "I propose unlimited toleration, or rather the destruction both of toleration and intoleration."[9] Shelley would substitute freedom for toleration, because toleration implies that the authority which practices it possesses also the power of arbitrarily choosing to be intolerant.

Shelley's ideas regarding political freedom are revealed to some extent in the latter part of the *Address*. His faith in the superiority of the force of reason to that of violence becomes one of the basic principles upon which he constructs his philosophy of politics:

We cannot believe just what we like, but only what we think to be true; for you cannot alter a man's opinion by beating or burning, but by persuading him that what you think is right, and this can be done by fair words and reason.[10]

It is upon this assumption, that people must believe only what they think to be true rather than what they would prefer to believe, that Shelley formulates policies which he thinks will aid the Irish people in their struggle for freedom.

Catholic Emancipation and the revocation of the Act of Union, the necessary first steps toward the establishment of political freedom for the Irish, are principal topics of the *Address*. The discussion of these objectives centers upon what Shelley considers to be the most suitable methods of achieving them. The Quaker doctrine that use of violence even in a just cause will inevitably lead to defeat is fervently endorsed. The French Revolution is a prime example of the catastrophe awaiting any worthy aim promoted by force:

[8] *Ibid.*, p. 44.
[9] *Ibid.*, p. 45.
[10] *Ibid.*, p. 44.

The cause which ... [the Revolutionists] vindicated was that of truth, but they gave it the appearance of a lie by using methods which will suit the purposes of liars as well as their own.[11]

He therefore urges the Irish people to assemble and speak their minds but warns against the undisciplined assembly, or mob, because it is inevitably leagued with violence.

There was some expectation in Ireland at the time of Shelley's visit that the Prince of Wales would remedy Irish grievances when he ascended the throne, for he had listened with apparent sympathy to the advice of Charles Fox, who favored the Irish cause. Shelley, aware of this development in the thinking of some of the advocates of Irish reform, warned against placing trust in the Prince. In doing so he anticipated, as Cameron observes, the position taken by Daniel O'Connell, who was at the time the most effective native leader of the movement for political reform in Ireland.[12]

Another important argument in the *Address* is the assertion that the English people as a whole do not, and would not, choose to maintain the conditions imposed upon Ireland by the English government. Shelley stresses the fact that only the upper, or governing, classes of England are responsible for Ireland's misery and that the general English population feel sympathy for the Irish people. Those who do not are the victims of their government's propaganda. The fact is that great masses of the English are almost as much victimized by their government as are the Irish.

As Shelley turns in the *Address* to those universal principles of politics which seem to be rooted in human nature, he abandons talk of Catholic Emancipation because it appears to him to be a foregone conclusion. It is merely preliminary to a genuine amelioration of Irish political conditions. Once Catholic Emancipation becomes fact, he observes, the Irish people "will be rendered equal to the people of England in their rights and

[11] *Ibid.*, p. 47.
[12] Cameron, *op. cit.*, p. 135, says "[Shelley] warns the Irish not to place all their trust in the Prince Regent and the Whigs (as Lord Fingall and the right wing of the Catholic Committee urged), and in this regard anticipates O'Connell, who did not challenge the Regent until June, 1812."

privileges, and will be in all respects, so far as concern the state, as happy".[13] This does not promise them much. The rich will remain too rich, the poor too poor. Riches and poverty alike debase the human spirit. Riches mean power, which corrupts, and poverty means servility, which degrades. Wealth and poverty are, therefore, not indexes to happiness. Happiness would be promoted "if . . . [rich and poor] could be prevailed upon to live equally like brothers. . . . But this can be done neither today nor tomorrow".[14] It is possible, however, to start instantly toward this goal, and the beginning must occur in the life of each person: "Mildness, sobriety, and reason are the effectual methods of forwarding the ends of liberty and happiness." [15] These virtues which must govern individual lives lead Shelley to enunciate his conception of politics:

Government is an evil; it is only the thoughtlessness and vices of men that make it a necessary evil. When all men are good and wise, government will of itself decay. . . . Society is produced by the wants, government by the wickedness, and a state of just and happy equality by the improvement and reason of man.[16]

The topic of individual reform, which will render government superfluous, is a favorite with Shelley; the remaining portion of the *Address* is given over to it. He argues, like Paine, Godwin, and others who pronounce government a necessary evil, that the

[13] *Shelley's Prose*, p. 50.
[14] *Ibid.*
[15] *Ibid.*
[16] *Ibid.*, p. 51. The conception of government as a necessary evil parallels that found in *Common Sense* (1776), in which Paine observes that society, the product of "our wants", came before government, the product of "our wickedness", and that society "promotes our happiness *positively* by uniting our affections", whereas government serves our welfare "*negatively* by restraining our vices" (*Basic Writings of Thomas Paine* (*Common Sense*), p. 1).

Godwin (*Enquiry Concerning Political Justice* (1798 edition), vol. I, p. 59) adopts Paine's theory, using his words: " 'Society and government . . . are different in themselves, and have different origins. Society is produced by our wants, and government by our wickedness. Society is in every state a blessing; government even in its best state but a necessary evil.' "

Shelley therefore could have got the idea through Godwin or from Paine directly. His conclusion that "a state of just and happy equality [is produced] by the improvement and reason of man" is unmistakenly Godwinian.

proper place for discipline is within the life of the individual citizen. Only here can sound government be established. This is an ideal which presupposes the perfectibility of human nature – perfectibility in the Godwinian sense of being infinitely capable of approaching perfection. It identifies the basic principles of government with the moral, personal virtues of honesty, justice, and wisdom but ignores methods of governing. The total effect of such a theory is the transference of the functions of government from an organization of people which we call a state to the individual, so that each person is a government complete within himself. There is nothing here of the concept of the social service, or welfare, state wherein the state is conceived of as an agency for doing those things for the individual which he cannot do for himself. The absence of this concept, however, is compensated for by the principle of the brotherhood of man.

The application of the principle of the brotherhood of man would act as a catalyst in promoting the ideal state. It implies a socialistic, if not communistic, view of property: "No friend would play false; no rents, no debts, no taxes, no frauds of any kind would disturb the general happiness." [17] The real sources of crime and vice have an economic foundation:

> I think those people ... are very silly ... who say that human nature is depraved; when at the same time wealth and poverty, those two great sources of crime, fall to the lot of a great majority of people; and when they see that people in moderate circumstances are always wise and good.[18]

If the young Shelley who wrote these lines oversimplified the psychological factors in human nature which produce crime by attributing them to the extremes of wealth and poverty, he must, nevertheless, be given credit for pointing the chief cause of the social ills of both England and Ireland at a time when any criticism of the distribution of wealth was looked upon as treasonable by his own government. Furthermore, he did not confuse values by elevating the material above the human and then arguing that the latter depend upon the former for their being

[17] *Shelley's Prose*, p. 52.
[18] *Ibid.*

— a trick employed by the conservative thinkers of his day, as now, to preserve the *status quo* in politics:

> People say that poverty is no evil; they have never felt it, or they would not think so; that wealth is necessary to encourage the arts – but are not the arts very inferior things to virtue and happiness? – the man would be very dead to all generous feelings who would rather see pretty pictures and statues than a million free and happy men.[19]

The conclusion of the *Address* is concerned primarily with freedom of assembly and press, without which there can be no free speech. Assembly and press are the weapons for effecting reform and barring abuses of political power. The natural right of free speech imposes responsibility: "The discussion of any subject is a right that you have brought into the world with your heart and tongue. ... it is fit that the governed should inquire into the proceedings of government."[20] Suggested topics of inquiry are the interests served by expansion of the British Empire, taxes levied upon the poor, and representation in the House of Commons. The *Address* ends with the promise of a proposal for an association aimed at repeal of the Union Act and removal of Catholic disabilities.

An Address to the Irish People marks important developments in Shelley's political principles. It deals with the specific political ills of Ireland but reveals their relationship to the political ills of the world. Of universal application is the discussion of the moral principles upon which political institutions must be founded.

The *Address* shows that Shelley at the age of nineteen espoused the political principles of republicanism, pacifism, and economic equalitarianism. These principles must rest upon the individual virtues of honesty, justice, and wisdom and the individual freedoms of speech, press, assembly, and religion. He was aware that freedom of religion implies separation of church and state, and his efforts to separate the moral principles of religion from their supernatural trappings would form the topic of a separate study. His political doctrines stem from an acceptance of the theory

[19] *Ibid.*
[20] *Ibid.*, p. 55.

that government is a necessary evil instituted to promote the happiness and welfare of the whole citizenry by protecting the inalienable, or natural, rights of the individual.

The second publication of Shelley's Irish mission, *Proposals for an Association of Philanthropists*, appeared on March 2, 1812. It aims to do the same things which he discussed doing in the *Address*. Catholic Emancipation remains a desirable first step toward political reform, but that by itself will hardly improve the lot of the Irish masses. Repeal of the Union Act, on the other hand, would be "a substantial benefit".[21] Both Catholic Emancipation and repeal can be considered only preliminary measures; true political reform depends upon widespread individual enlightenment.

Shelley hopes to establish a series of coordinated political organizations whose voice will be heard by those in authority. He again warns against secrecy and violence and sets general goals for the organizations to pursue but avoids specifying local projects:

I am ... indeterminate in my description of the association which I propose, because I conceive that an assembly of men meeting to do all the good that opportunity will permit them to do must be in its nature as indefinite and varying as the instances of human vice and misery that precede, occasion, and call for its institution.[22]

An association such as Shelley proposes would be the natural and recognized enemy of both the existing government and the priesthood. But opposition to these agencies is the very purpose of the association, because their misuse of power has created the need for it. The most important parts of the *Proposals*, however, are comments upon the rights of government, the French Revolution, and the Malthusian theory of population, for they enlarge to some extent upon Shelley's political doctrine. The problem of the constitutionality of the proposed associations leads to a discussion of the rights of government:

Government can have no rights: it is a delegation for the purpose of securing them to others. Man becomes a subject of government, not

[21] *Ibid.*, p. 62.
[22] *Ibid.*, p. 63.

that he may be in a worse, but that he may be in a better state than that of unorganized society. The strength of government is the happiness of the governed. All government existing for the happiness of others is just only so far as it exists by their consent, and useful only so far as it operates to their well-being.[23]

Concerning constitution Shelley says,

Constitution is to government what government is to law. Constitution may, in this view of the subject, be defined to be not merely something constituted for the benefit of any nation or class of people, but something constituted by themselves for their own benefit. The nations of England and Ireland have no constitution, because at no one time did the individuals that compose them constitute a system for the general benefit.[24]

These statements on government and constitution have their source in Paine's *Rights of Man:*

Man did not enter into society to become *worse* than he was before, nor to have less rights than he had before, but to have those rights better secured. His natural rights are the foundation of all his civil rights.[25]

The government of a free country, properly speaking, is not in the persons, but in the laws.

. . . .

A constitution is not the act of a government, but of a people constituting a government; and government without a constitution, is power without a right.[26]

Shelley would agree that England has a constitution if established customs and usages expressed in such compacts as the Magna Charta and the Bill of Rights conform to the meaning of a constitution, but he denies that this is what is meant by a constitution and therefore concludes:

[23] *Ibid.*, p. 64.
[24] *Ibid.*, pp. 64-65.
[25] *Basic Writings of Thomas Paine (Rights of Man)*, p. 37. Shelley acknowledges that the foundation of his political doctrine is that of the American and French revolutions: "it will appear that ... [my principles] have their origin from the discoveries in the sciences of politics and morals which preceded and occasioned the revolutions of America and France. It is with openness that I confess, nay with pride I assert, that they are so" (*Shelley's Prose*, p. 67).
[26] *Basic Writings of Thomas Paine (Rights of Man)*, pp. 176, 177.

> As ... in the true sense of the expression, the spot of earth on which we live is destitute of constituted Government, it is impossible to offend against its principles, or to be with justice accused of wishing to subvert what has no real existence.[27]

Shelley's view of the historical growth of the British constitution is opposed to that of Burke, who held that the established government was right and beyond the criticism of reason because it had grown into what it was without conforming to a reasoned plan. Hence Shelley concludes, "A philanthropic association has nothing to fear from the English constitution, but it may expect danger from its government." [28]

The *Proposals* indicate more clearly than do the previous writings that the system of politics envisaged is dictated by the concept of natural, inalienable, individual rights. The American and French revolutions grew out of this fundamental assumption. Shelley says,

> A man must have a right to do a thing before he can have a duty; this right must permit before his duty can enjoin him to act. Any law is bad which attempts to make it criminal to do what the plain dictates within the breast of every man tells him that he ought to do.[29]

The causes for the failure of the French Revolution, Shelley believes, are insufficient dissemination of ideas of the Encyclopedists and many of the promoters' infidelity to the ideals of liberty. A primary purpose of the proposed associations is the development of such leaders as those whose thought laid the intellectual foundation for the Revolution.

One other idea employed by the ruling classes to justify existing conditions and to scotch reform movements was the Malthusian doctrine of population. Thomas Malthus' *Essay on the Principle of Population* (1798) advanced the theory that populations tend to increase more rapidly than food supplies. Hence wars and disease will always remain the means of limiting populations to a size that can be fed. This became an excuse with the upper classes for inaction in the field of social welfare.

[27] *Shelley's Prose*, p. 65.
[28] *Ibid.*
[29] *Ibid.*, p. 66.

Ameliorate conditions for those who lived in poverty, and the number of poor would increase. Reform was thus made to appear futile.

Shelley's comments upon the Malthusian doctrine are a condemnation of the way in which it was being used rather than a penetrating analysis of its meaning and political implications. He exclaims, "Are we to be told that ... [war, vice, and misery] are remediless, because the earth would, in case of their remedy, be overstocked? ... Rare sophism!" [30]

It may be concluded, I believe, that the *Proposals*, had they been carried into effect, would have resulted in the formation of a political party. The general design of the associations which he suggests is that of modern democratic political parties. There would have been a central policy-making council, or association, directing and coordinating the activities of local associations. The central association would receive information from the subsidiary organizations as well as disseminate it to them. Hence the policy-making group would function in much the same way as national political committees, which gather information concerning the needs of various groups of citizens at the local level and then use it as a basis for drawing up a platform calculated to make known and secure those needs by strength of political opinion.

Before Shelley left Dublin on April 4, 1812, he published, but did not distribute, a broadside entitled *A Declaration of Rights*. It is a concise restatement of the arguments of *An Address to the Irish People* and the *Proposals for an Association of Philanthropists*. Since it contributes nothing new to our knowledge of his political thought of this period, it need not be considered here.

Biographical accounts of Shelley's disillusioning contact with Irish political leaders do not enhance our knowledge of his political doctrine but reveal that his approach to Irish political reform was more realistic than some parts of his published documents on the subject would suggest. His efforts to interest such patriots as John Curran and John Lawless in his project were practical. Furthermore, the experience of the Irish visit impressed upon Shelley some facts about human nature which reading and

[30] *Ibid.*, p. 68.

reason could not reveal. He discovered, for instance, that people's prejudices and habits of belief are often more dear to them than adventurous thought and activity which might lead to an improvement of their living conditions.[31] His introduction to Dublin's poverty also added another dimension to his knowledge:

> The appalling extent of the misery of the poor and of the injustice practiced by the rich came home to him in Dublin. He had known these facts intellectually before but never, in so intimate a sense, as an eye-witness. Such miserty implied a greater obduracy in the human heart than was to be softened by appeals to reason.[32]

In conclusion, it may be said that the Shelley who left Ireland early in April, 1812, espoused the following political dicta: (a) Government, a necessary evil, should be a delegation of powers by the governed, in whom rest the natural, inalienable rights of life, liberty, and the pursuit of happiness. (b) The institution of such a government implies the overthrow of existing aristocratic-monarchical forms, but the overthrow should be accomplished by the power of organized, enlightened public opinion rather than by violence. As a last resort, however, the use of force would be preferable to the collapse of the movement for reform. (c) The successful maintenance of a representative, republican form of government, once instituted, depends upon the equable distribution of goods, so that there can be no extremes of wealth and poverty. (d) All political reforms must rest ultimately upon individual moral virtues of honesty, courage, enlightenment, justice, and sympathy for one's fellow man.

A Letter to Lord Ellenborough (July, 1812), Shelley's next printed work, represents a continuation of the attempt to assume the role of practical politician. It bears somewhat obliquely upon political doctrine in that it is, in effect, a defense of Daniel Isaac Eaton's right as a citizen to freedom of speech and press. Eaton had been convicted in Lord Ellenborough's court and sentenced to the pillory and eighteen months in Newgate prison for having

---

[31] Shelley says in a letter to Elizabeth Hitchener, March 10, 1812, that "more hate me as a free-thinker than love me as a votary of freedom" (*Julian Works*, vol. VIII, p. 292).
[32] Carl Grabo, *The Magic Plant*, p. 80.

published Part Three of Paine's *Age of Reason*. The *Letter* is a protest against the conduct of the trial. Had it been published and circulated, Shelley would undoubtedly have been prosecuted, for he was under surveillance by governmental agents at the time. The significance of the *Letter* is that it attempts to make an object lesson of the Eaton trial. Lord Ellenborough allowed the prosecutor to prejudice the jury against Eaton by emphasizing that Eaton professed deistic rather than Christian views. Thus Eaton was convicted for religious belief rather than for having committed any crime. The government was guilty, in effect, of depriving him, and by implication the English citizenry at large, of freedom of speech and press.

Queen Mab, Shelley's first poem of literary significance, probably "left the press . . . in May or June 1813".[33] Ideas embodied in it are discussed at length in the "Notes". The major portion of poem and "Notes" constitutes an attack upon Christianity; the ideas are mainly those which Shelley had held "for several years already".[34] Notes of a political hue, however, contribute to Shelley's thought on economics and marriage. Even the comments on diet have a direct relation to political doctrine.

The note on diet appears separately as an essay, *A Vindication of Natural Diet* (1813). It contributes a minor point to Shelley's political thought. Men who are carnivorous violate a law of nature, because man is by nature a herbivorous creature. That man is naturally herbivorous is evident from the similarity between his physical structure and that of the herbivorous lower animals. Carnivorousness consequently produces the bad health in man which produces the evil of the mind that, in turn, renders governments a necessity, for evil is no more natural to man than carnivorousness. Laughable as Shelley's argument may be that there is a necessary connection between meat-eating and poor health, his contention that there is a close connection between poor health and a mind which refuses to adjust favorably to society is as solid now as ever. The latest development in medicine is the exploration of the relationship between mind and body

[33] White, *op. cit.*, vol. I, p. 291.
[34] *Ibid.*, vol. I, p. 292.

– psychosomatic medicine. It is now widely recognized that a person's physical health affects the way he thinks, and his mental attitude determines what sort of service he will require of his government.

The note to the lines

> And statesmen boast
> Of wealth! [35]

begins with a clearer statement of Shelley's idea of the nature of wealth and of the way in which existing government functions to preserve the misuse of wealth than we have got before. All real wealth is the product of man's labor. This stems ultimately from Adam Smith's *Wealth of Nations*. A corollary of this proposition is that emphasis upon a monetary system backed by the precious metals enables nonproducers of wealth to live in luxury at the expense of the workers. The aim of society becomes the possession rather than the production of wealth. The result is that a few acquire great surpluses and the many lack necessities. Those who can make ostentatious displays of riches are accorded prestige and respect whereas those who perform useful work are looked upon with contempt. The order of social values thus becomes inverted.

Shelley, like Adam Smith and others, makes utility the measure of the value of wealth. That which is useful contributes toward the happy and virtuous life. He would call the skills which produce useful products art. Hence the most fundamental art is cultivation of the land, without which society could not exist, and it is rendered the least rewarding of occupations under prevailing political institutions. Objects of art whose creation is made possible by accumulations of wealth are of secondary importance.[36]

The note concludes with the recognition that possession of wealth brings political power with it. For this reason established

---

[35] *Queen Mab*, V, lines 94-95, *Cambridge Works*, p. 16.
[36] This view appeared earlier in *An Address to the Irish People*: "People say ... that wealth is necessary to encourage the arts – but are not the arts very inferior things to virtue and happiness? – the man would be very dead to all generous feelings who would rather see pretty pictures and statues than a million free and happy men" (*Shelley's Prose*, p. 52).

EARLY OBJECTIVES OF POLITICAL REFORM 43

government is designed to maintain and promote the extreme economic imbalance between owners and producers of wealth to the detriment of both groups. Shelley's doctrine of economics at this period does not envisage the modern conception of an expanding economy. The solution to the problem of excessive wealth and poverty is simply the redistribution of existing wealth rather than an increase in the production and consumption of goods by improving working conditions and remuneration for laborers. The method of attaining this goal is the institution of a system of government which would make the great inequalities in distribution of wealth impossible. The result would be that all members of society would become producers of wealth, thus equalizing the distribution of power as well as the necessities of life.

The note on the line "Even love is sold",[37] attributes the evils of the relationship between the sexes to the moral code of the day. The marriage law, which supports the moral code, is charged with being the source of prostitution and with denying women's rights.[38] The irrevocability of legal marriage may force a life of misery upon either partner, or both. Hence marriage impinges upon individual liberty. Shelley's state would therefore abolish the marriage laws, and the union of men and women would be made to depend upon their mutual love and agreement.

On the Punishment of Death is a fragment of uncertain date.[39] There is general agreement, however, that it belongs to the period shortly following *Queen Mab*. With other fragmentary works on political doctrine it remained unpublished during Shelley's life and is considered at this point because it serves to round out Shelley's early political thought. The theme, as the title indicates, deals with the problem of legal punishment – its purpose and form. Shelley marshals a formidable array of arguments against the death penalty, not the least of which is a consideration of whether

---

[37] *Queen Mab*, V, line 189, *Cambridge Works*, p. 17.
[38] On this point Shelley draws heavily upon Mary Wollstonecraft's *A Vindication of the Rights of Woman*. See *Shelley's Prose*, Headnote, p. 115, for an account of this and other sources of the "Note".
[39] The date usually given is 1815. See White, *op. cit.*, vol. I, Note #32 of Chapter XIV, p. 704, on the dating of this and other fragmentary works.

death is a good or an evil. Other reasons for its abolition are that executions frequently make heroes of the victims when they die for a cause considered treasonable by established authority but popular with large numbers of people; punishment by death fails to deter those most likely to commit the crimes for which it is awarded because it displays the cheapness of life to them; the punishment of death serves in a measure as society's revenge upon the individual who breaks its laws, but revenge never served the ends of civilized justice; and finally, the cruelty of executions cultivates callousness and brutality throughout the social order. Shelley's arguments on this point are as sound now as they were in his own day, and they are slowly gaining acceptance by established governments.

III

POLITICAL TRACTS AFTER 1815

Shelley's work after 1815 centered upon the writing of poetry, but political reform remained an objective of prime importance to him. He wrote to Godwin on July 25, 1818, "I wish that I had health or spirits that would enable me to enter into public affairs, or that I could find words to express all that I feel and know."[1] Again on January 24, 1819, he wrote, "At present I write little else but poetry, and little of that. ... I consider Poetry very subordinate to moral and political science, and if I were well, certainly I should aspire to the latter."[2]

Despite a recognition that his talents were not adaptable to reform activities,[3] Shelley continued to express political views whenever circumstances seemed to invite comment. From the beginning of the growing crisis his confidence in the sound judgment and good sense of the people remained unshaken. He wrote Byron on November 20, 1816,

The whole fabric of society presents a most threatening aspect. What is most ominous of an approaching change is the strength which the popular party have suddenly acquired, and the importance which the violence of demagogues has assumed. But the people appear calm, and steady even under situations of great excitement; and reform may come without revolution.[4]

[1] *Julian Works*, vol. IX, p. 317.
[2] Shelley to Peacock, *ibid.*, vol. X, p. 21.
[3] Shelley to Leigh Hunt, December 8, 1816, *ibid.*, vol. IX, pp. 208-209: "I am undeceived in the belief that I have powers deeply to interest, or substantially to improve, mankind. How far my conduct and my opinions have rendered the zeal and ardour with which I have engaged in the attempt ineffectual, I know not."
[4] Shelley to Byron, *ibid.*, vol. IX, p. 204.

Early in 1817 he completed the pamphlet *A Proposal for Putting Reform to the Vote throughout the Kingdom*. It was published as by "The Hermit of Marlow" and distributed in March to "liberals with whom . . . [he] hoped . . . [it] might have practical results".[5] After conversations with Charles Ollier and Godwin on November 10 and 11 he wrote the tract *An Address to the People on the Death of the Princess Charlotte*. Completed on November 12, it was sent to Ollier for immediate publication. However, it is not known to have been printed before 1843.[6]

In 1819, the year of his greatest poetic productivity, we find that "At the very time when Shelley was writing *Prometheus Unbound* and *The Cenci* he also wrote his *Philosophical View of Reform*." [7] This lengthy but unfinished prose work, not published until 1920, is, in Shelley's words, "boldly but temperately written – and I think readable. It is intended for a kind of standard book for the philosophical reformers politically considered".[8] Additional evidence of his concern with the political unrest epitomized by the Manchester Massacre of August 16, 1819, is a series of poems written in a popular style and designed to censure the government and rally the oppressed in the cause of liberty. Like the *Philosophical View of Reform* they remained unpublished during his lifetime. Best known among them is *The Mask of Anarchy*, completed by the end of September and sent to Hunt for publication in the *Examiner*. The others are "Lines Written during the Castlereagh Administration", "Song: To the Men of England", "To Sidmouth and Castlereagh", "A New National Anthem", and "Sonnet: England in 1819". Two fragments, "To the People of England" and "What Men Gain Fairly", may be added to this group.

Though less inclined than formerly to rush into a political fray, in the fall of 1819 Shelley shows in letters from Italy an undiminished enthusiasm for reform. The critical events about which he was receiving news aroused fiery indignation:

---

[5] White, *op. cit.*, vol. I, p. 515.
[6] *Ibid.*, vol. I, p. 545.
[7] *Ibid.*, vol. II, p. 144.
[8] Shelley to Hunt, May 26, 1820, *Julian Works*, vol. X, p. 172.

The same day that your letter came, came the news of the Manchester Work, and the torrent of my indignation has not yet done boiling in my veins. I wait anxiously [to] hear how the country will express its sense of this bloody, murderous oppression of its destroyers.[9]

Shelley shared the widespread fear that the Manchester riot and other incidents of unrest were the prelude to a bloody revolution. The real danger from the pressures for reform was that the government might precipitate a civil war by irresponsible acts of violence:

I fear that in England things will be carried violently by the rulers, and that they will not have learned to yield in time to the spirit of the age. The great thing to do is to hold the balance between popular impatience and tyrannical obstinacy; to inculcate with fervour both the right of resistance and the duty of forbearance.[10]

How defendants against government prosecution fared in the courts served as a barometer to approaching civil strife. Any evidence of the courts' refusal to impose harsh penalties against those accused of crimes by the government simply because they were accused showed strength for the forces of reform. Shelley was therefore greatly encouraged upon receiving word from Peacock early in 1819 of the acquittal of four men accused of forging bank notes because the only evidence against them was that of hired informers:

Your news about the Banknote trials is excellent good. Do I recognise in it the influence of Cobbet? You don't tell me what occupies Parliament? I know you will laugh at my demand, and assure me that it is indifferent.[11]

On November 3, 1819, Shelley wrote a letter in defense of Richard Carlile and sent it to Hunt for publication.[12] In October Carlile had been fined 5,500 pounds, forced to give 1,200 pounds as security for good behavior during life, and sentenced to three years in prison. His crime was "blasphemy in publishing Palmer's

---

[9] Shelley to Ollier, September 6, 1819, *ibid.*, vol. X, p. 82.
[10] Shelley to Hunt, November (no day given), 1819, *ibid.*, vol. X, pp. 130-131.
[11] Shelley to Peacock, January 24, 1819, *ibid.*, vol. X, p. 20.
[12] See *Julian Works*, vol. X, pp. 105-119.

Principles of Nature and Paine's *Age of Reason*".[13] Shelley's argument, like that for Peter Finnerty earlier, was that Carlile had not received a fair trial. His jury had been a group of clergymen instead of his peers. Unorthodox religious belief was what had really convicted him rather than evidence of criminal activity. He had been denied equal justice because the government had failed to prosecute and convict more prominent individuals, such as Sir William Drummond, William Godwin, and Jeremy Bentham, whose religious beliefs were equally unorthodox. The effect of the trial was to strengthen the power of an established church which acted as an aid to the government in stifling criticism. Hunt did not publish the letter, an effective legal argument in behalf of freedom of thought and speech, because publication would probably have led to his imprisonment.

A Proposal for Putting Reform to the Vote throughout the Kingdom (1817) is devoted, by and large, to a scheme for securing an expression as to "whether the majority of the adult individuals of the United Kingdom of Great Britain and Ireland desire or no a complete representation in the legislative assembly".[14] This appears to be an odd proposal, for it is in substance a suggestion that the people be asked whether or not they want a Parliament whose members must institute reforms they have been fighting for. What Shelley envisages is a petition to Parliament, signed by a majority of "adult individuals", for a reform of the method of selecting members of the House of Commons. The membership would be made to represent the people rather than property.

It is unlikely that Shelley expected Parliament to respond to a petition, whatever the number of signatures, by enacting a measure which would turn its members out of office. Parliament would adopt such a radical reform only if it feared the consequences of a bloody revolution less than the risk of precipitating one. Efforts to enforce harsh laws against its critics at the time (March, 1817) gave no evidence that Parliament was, or was likely to become, of this frame of mind. The petition, however, might serve as a stimulus to peaceful reform. It would function as a device for

[13] White, *op. cit.*, vol. II, p. 166.
[14] *Shelley's Prose*, p. 159.

informing and uniting. Its presentation to the people would emphasize that the real goal of political reform was representative government rather than the expedient redress of grievances. Its signers would be united in, and committed to, the cause. Viewed in this way the proposal is sound.

If a majority should be unwilling to go on record as favoring a change in the method of selecting the members of the House of Commons, the advocates of reform would see not only the uselessness but also the danger of continuing their efforts. Real progress could come only as the result of enlightened and resolute public opinion. On this point Shelley's great respect for the principle of majority rule is made clear:

we should be guilty of the great crime which I have conditionally imputed to the House of Commons if after unequivocal evidence that it was the national will to acquiesce in the existing system we should ... excite the minority to disturb this decision.[15]

The chief merit of the scheme is that it offered an approach to the problem of securing political reforms upon which all the advocates of reform could agree. Representative government was the basic issue. Beside it, as Shelley points out, other proposed reforms, such as qualifications for voting and the calendar of Parliamentary meetings, were of secondary importance, though they were the cause of dissension among leaders in the movement.

The government's readiness in 1817 to suppress reform activities probably made the execution of Shelley's plan impossible. Had it been carried out, it might have been a first step toward popular representation in the government. Confronted with a petition bearing the signatures of the majority of the adult citizenry, Parliament would likely have proceeded with more caution in the exercise of repressive measures. It might well have attempted to appease public opinion by reversing some of its tyrannical policies. Step by step the united majority could then pursue reforms leading to a government responsible to the people.

The conservativeness of *A Proposal for Putting Reform to the Vote* is reflected in the concluding remarks on the frequency of

[15] *Ibid.*, pp. 159-160.

Parliamentary meetings, suffrage, and the aristocracy. Annual meetings of Parliament are advocated because they "would familiarize men with liberty by disciplining them to an habitual acquaintance with its forms".[16] Immediate adoption of universal suffrage, an ideal objective, would be dangerous because of the "present unprepared state of public knowledge and feeling".[17] The vote should not be given even to the entire male population. Only "those who register their names as paying a certain small sum in *direct taxes* ought, at present, to send members to Parliament".[18] The abolition of the aristocracy, like full extension of the franchise, should wait upon the arrival of the masses at political maturity.

An Address to the People on the Death of the Princess Charlotte (1817) is another instance of Shelley's penetrating political thought. It reflects his keen sense of the dramatic in the turn of events. The cause of reform had become identified to some extent with the expectation that the Princess Charlotte would succeed her father to the throne. Though young and without experience in affairs of state, she was popular with the people and was believed to favor reforms which "many of the best minds in England felt must be achieved if a revolution was to be averted".[19] When she died in childbirth on November 6, 1817, the future looked even darker than it had before. The ensuing national mourning prompted the writing of the tract.

Public mourning is an occasion for reflection:

It were well done . . . that men should mourn for any public calamity which has befallen their country or the world, though it be not death.[20]

The calamity which Shelley discusses involves death, the execution on November 7 of three laborers who had been convicted of taking part in a rebellion, but is not merely the punishment itself. It is, rather, the part played by the government as instigator of the disorder in which they were involved. A government agent had promoted the outbreak so as to provide a pretext for the use

[16] *Ibid.*
[17] *Ibid.*
[18] *Ibid.*
[19] White, *op. cit.*, vol. I, p. 544.
[20] *Shelley's Prose*, p. 164.

of force. This maneuver was calculated to display the strength of the government and through fear prevent the people from protesting against desperate living conditions. The enormous national debt, incurred through a method of anticipating taxes by loans, is the source of the depressed standard of living:

> The effect of this debt is to produce such an unequal distribution of the means of living as saps the foundation of social union and civilized life. It creates a double aristocracy, instead of one which was sufficiently burdensome before, and gives twice as many people the liberty of living in luxury and idleness on the produce of the industrious and the poor.[21]

The new aristocracy, unlike the old, are "petty piddling slaves who have gained a right to the title of public creditors, either by gambling in the funds, or by subserviency to government, or some other villainous trade".[22] The two aristocracies double the burden on the laborer. He now "gains no more ... by working sixteen hours a day than he gained before by working eight".[23] The discontent and disaffection arising from these conditions are reflected in the demand for representative government. Parliament, seeing the threat to its power, responded by murdering British liberty, which, like the Princess, was "young, innocent, and lovely".[24] It is, therefore, for dead liberty that England should mourn.

A Philosophical View of Reform is a fragment of approximately 20,000 words. Written in 1819-1820, it remained unpublished for a hundred years. Yet it is, perhaps, Shelley's most important political work. Though fragmentary, it is a final statement of his views. Only the *Defence of Poetry*, written in 1821 and published posthumously in 1840, comes later, and as a commentary on politics it has little significance. Though relatively unknown before its publication in 1920,[25] *A Philosophical View of Reform*

[21] *Ibid.*, p. 166.
[22] *Ibid.*
[23] *Ibid.*
[24] *Ibid.*, p. 168.
[25] Edward Dowden published a condensation of the work in *Transcripts and Studies* (1888).

provides a discussion of ideas which had evolved from a short but concentrated life of study and political activity during the critical decade beginning with 1812. It serves as an aid to interpreting some of Shelley's major poetry.[26] Shelley says (see above, p. 46), "It is intended for a kind of standard book for the philosophical reformers politically considered." Lacking practical influence upon reformers, the work is valuable as a compendium of political thought.

The work begins with the observation that only those in authority who imagine their personal interest to be identified with maintaining the *status quo* in English political affairs do not acknowledge the necessity of reform. This is a view which inevitably emerges from events of the day. Conditions which impress this view result from the use of schemes for the abridgment of individual liberties. These schemes have a long history. The most successful of them was the Roman Empire. Succeeding ones, though smaller, served the purposes of tyranny as well. The Roman Catholic Church, allied with various dynasties, perverted the system of liberty and equality which Jesus taught, to support oppression. For some time the Italian republics and city governments successfully resisted the surrounding tyranny. Their resistance was inevitably crushed. Another, the Reformation, inevitably developed. Though an imperfect reform, it secured enough freedom to produce the republics of Holland and Switzerland. In England the aroused spirit of liberty released the extraordinary energy of intellectual power which is evidenced in the writings of the age of Elizabeth and James I. Liberty stood as both a cause and a further effect of the flowering of the arts.

The vicissitudes of the continuing struggle between the forces of liberty and oppression in England brought the overthrow of

[26] Dowden writes (*Transcripts and Studies*, second edition (1896), p. 41), "it seems desirable that those persons ... who would make themselves acquainted with the total achievement, in all its breadth and variety, of Shelley's extraordinary thirty years, should, in common with me, possess some acquaintance with a piece of writing belonging to his period of full maturity, which may be viewed in a certain sense as a prose comment on those poems that anticipate, as does the 'Prometheus Unbound', a better and happier life of man."

monarchy, the temporary establishment of a commonwealth, the execution of Charles I, the restoration of Charles II, and finally the Revolution of 1688. The outcome, represented in the Revolution settlement of 1689, produced few material benefits for the oppressed, but a significant constitutional principle was acknowledged: the people had the legal right to change their government. A parallel consequence of the Reformation was the recognition that every person has the inalienable right of protesting against religious dogmas which seem false to him, including those propounded by the leaders of the Reformation.

Political philosophy and the physical sciences progressed with equal rapidity in the seventeenth and eighteenth centuries:

> The result of the labors of the political philosophers has been the establishment of the principle of utility as the substance and liberty and equality as the forms, according to which the concerns of human life ought to be administered.[27]

Under the stimulus of astonishing advances in the physical sciences commerce rose to unprecedented heights and thus provided further sources of knowledge. The new access to power should have benefitted the human race tremendously, but paradoxically it increased misery, owing to a vicious social structure:

> Modern society is ... an engine assumed to be for useful purposes, whose force is by a system of subtle mechanism augmented to the highest pitch, but which, instead of grinding corn or raising water, acts against itself and is perpetually wearing away or breaking to pieces the wheels of which it is composed.[28]

The United States of America, though not an ideal republic, provides "the first practical illustration of the new philosophy".[29] A representative government, it has no king, aristocracy, or established church. It is distinguished from all other governments by having a constitution which provides for its own amendment according to the expressed will of the people. These features, rather than situation, are the strength of the American state and the source of prosperity and happiness of the people.

[27] *Shelley's Prose*, p. 234.
[28] *Ibid.*, pp. 233-234.
[29] *Ibid.*, p. 234.

Shelley admired the government of the United States because it epitomized the principles which he had advocated from the beginning of his study of politics. The lack of a king and an aristocracy removed the chief source of corruption in government. The separation of church and state was a safeguard against the abridgment of liberty in the name of institutional religion. There was no need for maintaining a costly standing army and a Court of Chancery, the agencies for perpetuating the power of hereditary rulers. Even the system of representation, though open to abuses, is the only practicable means of democracy in a large state:

[The United States] has no false representation, whose consequences are captivity, confiscation, infamy, and ruin, but a true representation. The will of the many is represented by the few in the assemblies of legislation and by officers of the executive entrusted with the administration of the executive power almost as directly as the will of one person can be represented by the will of another.[30]

The French Revolution was a result of the same state of public opinion in Europe that in America had separated the colonies from England. Its failure was the product of French institutions. Unlike the colonists, whose customs and political institutions embodied some elements of self rule prior to the war for independence, the French had no traditions which would serve as a transition from despotism to a freedom for which they were unprepared. The Revolution was only a partial failure, however. Despite the reign of terror, the usurpation of Napoleon, and the restoration of the Bourbons, important gains were made:

[France's] legislative assemblies are in a certain limited degree representations of the popular will, and the executive power is hemmed in by jealous laws. ... abuses were abolished which never since have dared show their face.[31]

A survey of world events and conditions indicates, to Shelley, that the spirit of freedom is stirring in Germany, Spain, South America, India, the Turkish Empire, Syria, Arabia, the West Indies. Obstacles to liberty range from the oppression in Spain to

---

[30] *Ibid.*
[31] *Ibid.*, p. 236.

slavery in the West Indies. Some countries have acquired a measure of popular rule. There are presages of revolution in countries suffering from the worst of despotism. Even "The great monarchies of Asia cannot ... remain unshaken by the earthquake which shatters to dust the 'mountainous strongholds' of the tyrants of the western world".[32]

Shelley's interpretation of history leads to the conclusion that the human race is renewing the progress which was interrupted by the overthrow of Greek civilization:

Such is a slight sketch of the general condition of the human race to which they have been conducted after the obliteration of the Greek republics by the successful external tyrany of Rome – its internal liberty having been first abolished – and by those miseries and superstitions consequent upon this event which compelled the human race to begin anew its difficult and obscure career of producing, according to the forms of society, the great portion of good.[33]

Shelley examines the rise of the current political crisis in England against this brief historical background. In 1819 almost everyone except the ruling classes was aware of the necessity and desirability of a change in government. The need for reform grew in proportion to the decline of popular representation in Parliament. Suffrage diminished relatively with increases in population. From 1641 to 1688 the ratio of those excluded from suffrage to those having it increased from eight to one to twenty to one.[34] A factor contributing to the lack of popular representation was the great influence exercised by members of the House of Lords upon selection of members of the House of Commons.[35] The membership of Commons was in effect chosen by the Lords. This arrangement was not detrimental to the welfare of the nation as a whole in 1641, when commoners and peers were united against Charles I and his agents. Circumstances which enforced this

[32] Ibid., p. 238.
[33] Ibid., p. 239.
[34] The source of the statistics is not given.
[35] The election of Shelley's father, Sir Timothy, to the House of Commons in 1790 is an example of this. Sir Timothy first sought a seat in Commons at the instigation of the Duke of Norfolk, whose interests he supported throughout his long tenure in office (see above, Chapter I, p. 14).

union finally disappeared with the advent of the Revolution of 1688 and the establishment of William III on the throne in 1689. The result was that the struggle for political power which had been waged between the Crown and Parliament was settled in favor of Parliament. Control of Parliament remained, as before, in the hands of the aristocracy and was maintained as a hereditary right. The inflexibility of institutions further disfranchised the growing population.

The new political era which began in 1688 produced the "despotism of the oligarchy of party".[36] With the help of the people the aristocracy had severely limited the powers of the Crown. Parliamentary ministers now began to exercise executive authority that had been the king's. They were members of the controlling party, or faction, and served as its leaders. The policies pursued were designed to consolidate gains against the encroachment of both the Crown and the people and to benefit the economic interests of the aristocracy. The rise in power and fortune of the rich and decline in living standard of the population at large testified to the efficiency of the ministerial system which was devised. The Lords and their ministers were able to keep their self-serving activities from public view by acting in the name of the king.

A primary device for accomplishing the purposes of the oligarchy of party was public credit in the form of paper money, an innovation of the reign of William III. The government destroyed the stability of the monetary system, which was based upon gold, by printing more paper money, or promissory notes, than could be backed with gold. The holders of paper money were prevented by law from redeeming it in gold or some other universally acceptable medium of exchange. It was declared legal tender. The resulting fluctuations in the purchasing power of money served the interests of speculators at the expense of the producers of goods. The rise in prices brought additional riches to the wealthy and thus increased the demand for luxuries. It increased the laborer's working day beyond human endurance. The necessities that could formerly be secured for eight or ten

[36] *Shelley's Prose*, p. 243.

hours of work per day now required twenty. The workingman's plight became desperate. The aged and the sickly were forced to work or starve. Children were put to work to help support their families.

Another consequence of public credit was the creation of a new aristocracy of "attorneys and excisemen and directors and government pensioners, usurers, stock jobbers, country bankers, with their dependents and descendants".[37] This aristocracy did not replace, but supplemented, hereditary aristocracy, whose fiscal policies created it. Lacking the qualities of style and manner which lent some dignity to the landed, hereditary aristocracy, it had no redeeming features. The two aristocracies, constituting a class of drones in the social order, became an unbearable burden upon laborers, the source of all real wealth.

The conditions fostered by the government were contrary to the purpose government ought to serve: "all classes of society, excepting those within the privileged pale, . . . [are] singularly unprosperous", whereas "public happiness is the substance and the end of political institution".[38] A share of the nation's wealth sufficient to make possible a moderate degree of happiness is the right of every citizen. A government that does not enforce this principle must be reformed.

An approach to the problem of improving the condition of the poor envisaged by the aristocracy derived from the Malthusian dictum that population tends to outrun food supply. Malthus suggested that the poor decrease the birth rate by abstaining from sexual intercourse. The withholding of payments authorized by the poor laws could be used to enforce this program. Shelley scorns the injustice and absurdity of this proposal.

Reform should constitute the recovery by the people of former liberties and privileges and the establishment of some form of government which would make these rights secure. Essentials of reform would include the abolition of the national debt, and of sinecures, tithes, and a favored religion. The standing army would be disbanded and the jury system extended. Justice would be

[37] *Ibid.*, p. 245.
[38] *Ibid.*, pp. 246-247.

made available to everybody by being made cheap, certain, and swift.

The national debt resulted chiefly from wars fought against America and France in the interest of the wealthy classes and without real popular support. It does not represent an obligation contracted with the approval, and for the benefit, of the population at large. It is owed to the wealthy classes and is secured by the land and other property which they own. The enormous interest on it is paid with tax money that comes mainly from the laboring classes, who own little property. The aristocracy's control of the economy depends upon its continuation. It serves as a device for extorting from wage earners money which is paid as interest to the rich from whom the government borrowed. The effects bring ruin to most of the people. Economic justice demands that the principal be paid. How to do this is not so difficult a problem as is pretended: "The property of the rich is mortgaged . . . let the mortgagee foreclose." [39]

Paying the principal by foreclosure would involve governmental seizure of property. To do this equitably would require the valuation of all property according to a standard from which the present value of the debt could be adjusted to its value at the time it was contracted. The price of corn might serve as the standard. From the adjusted property valuations a judgment could be made as to how much property each owner must give up to satisfy his obligation. Since the property owners are both the lenders and the borrowers, settlement would be accomplished by adjusting their claims as creditors against their obligations as debtors. They would settle the debt among themselves, and the wage earners would be relieved from the burden of paying half of their meager earnings as taxes to satisfy the interest on it. The need for settling the national debt in this way is urgent: "One of the first acts of a reformed government would undoubtedly be an effectual scheme for compelling . . . [persons of property] to compromise their debt between themselves." [40]

Related to the problem of equitably paying the national debt

[39] *Ibid.*, p. 249.
[40] *Ibid.*, p. 250.

and of taxing capital to meet public emergencies is the problem of claims to property. The method of acquisition determines the priority of claim. The most forceful claim belongs to those who acquire property for "labor, industry, economy, skill, genius, or any similar powers honorably and innocently exerted".[41] Thus acquired, property does not accumulate into great fortunes, and political institutions ought to safeguard the right of persons holding it to dispose of it as they choose. Inheritance rights to such property may be guaranteed without danger of promoting extremes of wealth and poverty. Accidental increases in its value would be offset by accidental depletions. Though claims become weakened by descent, disposing of property by will is a privilege necessarily linked with existing forms of domestic life.

The fortunes of the aristocracy and the "great fund-holders" are accumulations of another kind of property. It necessarily "has its foundation in usurpation, or imposture, or violence".[42] Claims to landed estates derive from grants of feudal lords whose method of acquisition was conquest and oppression, or from the repossession by the nation of property which had belonged to "the ancient Catholic clergy", or from "the products of patents and monopolies".[43] In more recent times fortunes are amassed by "taking advantage of a fictitious paper currency to obtain an unfair power over labor and the fruits of labor."[44] Unlike claims to legitimate property, claims to this species are strengthened through inheritance. Consequently, large fortunes tend to snowball.

In the absence of emergencies for which some of the national resources must be appropriated, private claims to immense accumulations of property may be allowed if their existence evidences "an overbalance of public advantage".[45] Any emergency, such as that created by the national debt, must be financed by a tax on capital, which would fall with least injustice upon those whose possessions were not secured from labor and skill or from

[41] *Ibid.*
[42] *Ibid.*, p. 251.
[43] *Ibid.*
[44] *Ibid.*
[45] *Ibid.*, p. 252.

the profits and savings of labor and skill. The great fortunes, built upon conquest, oppression, monopoly, and manipulation of the monetary system, "can only be called property in a modified sense".[46] Claims to them, lacking the forcefulness of claims to property derived from labor and skill, would therefore be the first to be abrogated.

The argument that the burden of paying the national debt should be left to future generations, beneficiaries of the operations for which the debt was created, has no validity. History shows that emergencies are claimed for each generation. New debts would be created. Consequently, delaying payment would bring an increase in principal and interest, in the number of idle rich, in demands for luxuries, in prices, and in the number of working hours necessary for producers of goods to make a living. Present injustices and hardships would be multiplied and intensified for posterity.

Universal suffrage is a principle which is fundamental to individual liberty. Yet its immediate institution in England would be tantamount to the establishment of a republic, an event which would almost certainly be attended by violence. The people, having acquired sovereignty, would see the consequence of doctrines which the demagogues employ. They would therefore be impelled to abolish monarchy and aristocracy, to level inordinate wealth, and to distribute agricultural and uncultivated lands. This would likely precipitate a civil war which would retard the cause of freedom by making the continuation of "military habits ... already introduced by our tyrants" [47] a necessity. The purposes of a republican form of government, however admirable, would thus be defeated. A program of education should precede efforts to institute universal suffrage. Slow but sure progress would follow the spread of knowledge and understanding of human rights and of proper political objectives.

Political reform must be predicated upon "the natural equality of men, not with relation to their property but to their rights".[48]

---

[46] Ibid.
[47] Ibid., p. 253.
[48] Ibid.

POLITICAL TRACTS AFTER 1815   61

The doctrine of equal possessions among men is moral rather than political. Though moral and political principles, ideally considered, cannot be separated, the moral principle of equal possessions is practicably unattainable. It should be made an objective toward which political institutions tend.

Popular representation in the House of Commons might be achieved by dividing Great Britain and Ireland into five hundred "electoral departments or parishes" of 40,000 citizens each. Since women, who should not yet be given the right of suffrage, children, and persons under age constitute two thirds of the population, the eligible voters of each electoral district would number only 13,333. With each district electing one member to Commons, the membership of that body would be fixed at five hundred. Qualified citizens throughout the empire would assemble on a designated day to exercise their right of suffrage.

Voting by ballot is to be condemned for two reasons. As a system of electing representatives it is too mechanical. Voters and candidates should meet in an assembly. Personal acquaintance would promote understanding between elector and elected. Secondly, the user of the ballot would be guided by dishonorable motives because his vote would be kept secret. He would not have to account publicly for his choice. The true purposes of government can be served only when the light of publicity is brought to bear upon the exercise of sovereignty.

Shelley's arguments condemning the secret ballot would be valid for only a small, ideal democracy. They are impractical for a country such as England. Having voters and candidates meet to discuss issues is a worthy objective. The exchange of ideas between candidates and voters in a forum is fundamental to the democratic process, but a forum is not a substitute for the secret ballot. Each voter would have to have the wisdom and articulateness of a philosopher and the courage to be independent if he were made publicly accountable for the way he votes. Otherwise, coercion and intimidation would put an end to free elections.

The advocates of reform should be contented with any reform however limited, that the existing government might introduce. Once begun, reforms could be resolutely pursued, step by step, and gradually realized. This would, in fact, be the best way because the people would not suddenly have to exercise rights and fulfill responsibilities for which they were not prepared. Suffrage for small property holders and triennial parliaments are measures which all reformers should accept as a satisfactory beginning. To disdain them, or any other limited reforms which might be proffered by the government, because they are small would be to risk disaster in the ensuing struggle to secure greater benefits.

If Parliament should refuse to initiate any reform – and it seemed likely that this would be its course – Shelley would favor the institution of universal suffrage and equal representation, whatever the consequences. This would have to be done in defiance of the government, which controlled the army and other enforcing agencies. The best weapon of the side of reform would be enlightenment, unity, and enthusiasm for the cause. Matched against an overwhelming majority possessing these attributes, an intelligent ruling minority would yield without precipitating civil war.

Since the people, inured to poverty, lack political knowledge of how to oppose their oppressors without resorting to violence, the true patriots of England must work tirelessly to educate them and to rally them to objectives which all would support enthusiastically. Open confederations rather than secret associations are the means of doing this. Government interference with meetings by force of arms should be met with passive resistance. Either flight or the use of force would invite massacre. The soldier would fire upon those who tried to escape, and a sense of his own danger would cause him to massacre those who offered resistance. Passive resistance would be effective because the soldiers, themselves Englishmen, would not slaughter their unarmed compatriots whose resistance was limited to a refusal to disperse or submit to their authority. Surprise at such a reception might cause them to see that they were being made the instruments of tyranny, desert government service, and join with their intended victims.

Passive resistance can be used to achieve reform and preclude further struggle only if it is uniform and nationwide in scope. The depressed and abject state of the people, which is, perhaps, the strongest evidence of the urgent need for reform, may prevent the kindling of the impulse to passive resistance. Reform too long delayed will allow the English people to sink into an "incurable supineness" resembling that of the Asians. Maneuvers which should be used to supplement passive resistance include the testing of intrenched authority by an aroused and active public opinion, suits in courts of common law challenging the government's right to impose taxes, and petitions to Parliament. Any questionable exercise of authority by the government ought to be defied. This would lead to prosecutions which would serve to bring public opinion into focus: "No law or institution can last if this opinion be distinctly pronounced against it." [49] Any concessions by the government which these stratagems might stimulate should be the signal for a pause in the campaign for reform. The people should be urged to demand additional rights only after they have learned the proper exercise of those which they have already secured. It is better that adequate reforms should be twenty years in coming than that their sudden acquisition should precipitate civil war.

Insurrection as a means of establishing reforms is a last resort: "The right of insurrection is derived from the employment of armed force to counteract the will of the nation." [50] There is grave danger that war will defeat the purpose for which it is undertaken because history reveals that war and tyranny play into each other's hands. Armies are the ready-made tools of oppression because they represent immense concentrations of power in the hands of a few commanders. The motives for which wars are fought easily become identified with those of their leaders. The advantages gained in the French Revolution were subverted in this way. The waging of war and the cultivation of the sentiment of reason and justice are incompatible. Insurrection, despite the risks, is preferable to the ultimate moral and political degradation which will arrive if the struggle for reform is abandoned.

Victory for the people, by whatever means, will not of itself

[49] *Ibid.*, p. 258.
[50] *Ibid.*, p. 259.

solve many important problems. After the people have put their representatives in office and have assumed control of public affairs,

there will remain the great task of accommodating all that can be preserved of ancient forms with the improvements of the knowledge of a more enlightened age in legislation, jurisprudence, government and religious and academical institutions.[51]

Victory must follow above all else the course of magnanimity rather than revenge, for revenge is a characteristic of savagery, not civilization.

Shelley left the work unfinished at this point.

A Philosophical View of Reform is both a summation and a culmination of Shelley's political thought. In it we find an approval of republicanism and a denunciation of monarchy that date back to his Oxford days. There is an advocacy of abolishing a favored state religion and of achieving reform by open political organization employing passive resistance, that appeared in the Irish pamphlets (1812). The view that the strongest claims to wealth belong to the laborers, who create it, whereas the government, which should protect their claims, promotes extremes of wealth and poverty by practices which deprive the laborers of the fruit of their labor, found expression in *Queen Mab* and the "Notes" (1813). The argument that representative government is of necessity the basic aim of reform, though universal suffrage, an ideal goal, should not be instituted until the people become educated to the responsibilities it would place upon them, appeared in *A Proposal for Putting Reform to the Vote throughout the Kingdom* (1817). The necessity of paying the national debt, which, together with innovations in the monetary system, created a second aristocracy, or class of drones in the social order, and thus doubled an already unbearable burden upon workers, was pointed out in *An Address to the People on the Death of the Princess Charlotte* (1817). The work presents no ideas that Shelley has not advanced before. It is conclusive evidence, despite its fragmentary character, that the major tenets of his

[51] *Ibid.*, p. 260.

political thought were the same in 1820 as when he sailed for Ireland in 1812.

Some changes, however, are discernible. They are changes in emphasis rather than in character. Shelley says, for example, that "Morals and politics can only be considered as portions of the same science".[52] This agrees with his earlier statements. In a letter of January 7, 1812, to Elizabeth Hitchener (see above, Chapter I, Footnote # 2, p. 12) he wrote, "Southey says Expediency ought to [be] made the ground of politics but not of morals. I urged that the most fatal error that ever happened in the world was the separation of political and ethical science." Again in *A Declaration of Rights* (1812) he said, "Expediency is inadmissible in morals. Politics are only sound when conducted on principles of morality. They are, in fact, the morals of the nations." [53] He now places emphasis upon the relationship between principle and practice:

> That equality in possessions which Jesus Christ so passionately taught is a moral rather than political truth and is such as social institutions cannot without mischief inflexibly secure. . . . Equality in possessions must be the last result of the utmost refinements of civilization; it is one of the conditions of that system of society towards which with whatever hope of ultimate success, it is our duty to tend.[54]

The conception of a moral principle, or ideal, as a goal beyond reach but toward which society ought to move constantly is not stressed in the early political writings. There is, rather, a tendency to picture an ideal society as an actuality. Those portions of the Irish pamphlets that picture an ideal state in which sobriety, reason, and benevolence govern the lives of a free citizenry, and the conclusion of *Queen Mab*, which reveals the secrets of the future, provide illustrations of this. In 1820 it is still Shelley's great delight to represent ideals graphically, but we must turn to the poetry to find the representations.

The cautiousness of Shelley's proposals for reform is apparent in all of his works. From the beginning of his career he advocates

---

[52] *Ibid.*, p. 253.
[53] *Ibid.*, p. 71.
[54] *Ibid.*, pp. 253-254.

open, non-violent methods of securing needed changes in political institutions. He consistently emphasizes the desirability of securing a few reforms at a time, but the early works stress the changes themselves. He now writes (see quoted passage above, p. 64) of "the great task of accommodating all that can be preserved of ancient forms with ... the knowledge of a more enlightened age". Stress is placed upon preservation as well as upon change.

A Philosophical View of Reform is in essence a plan for preventing a rebellion which seemed inevitable. If there is a complement of radicalism in it, it is, as White suggests,[55] the plan for payment of the national debt. Shelley would liquidate the debt by direct, confiscatory taxation of the rich. Though this proposal would be considered radical by most democratic governments today, his argument for its fairness stands upon the same principle as does the widely used graduated income tax: people should be taxed in accordance with their ability to pay.

Special confiscatory taxes, such as inheritance taxes on large fortunes, are often levied by present-day governments. The upper brackets of the graduated income tax are usually confiscatory in effect. When misused, such taxes are discriminatory and become weapons of political tyranny for the economic destruction of certain classes or groups. Wisely formulated and administered, they serve to reduce the imbalance between rich and poor and to improve the general distribution of wealth, purposes advocated by Shelley.

Shelley's emphasis in *A Philosophical View of Reform* upon specific reforms and the lack of stress upon political theory represent a retreat from, if not a denial of, his earlier doctrine that government has power to produce only evil and is a necessary evil only because men are not sufficiently enlightened to live together without it. The pamphlets of the Irish venture do not deny that evils would coexist with a reformed government. They advocate the awakening of men's minds by argument and persuasion, and convey the impression that in the resulting enlightenment government would become an unnecessary evil and

[55] White, *op. cit.*, vol. II, p. 149.

vanish. In *A Philosophical View of Reform* emphasis is placed upon the necessity of getting social good out of reformed institutions by making them expressions of an informed and politically active citizenry. The work amounts to an avowal that a reformed government would produce good, not evil. It is an acknowledgment that a government in which sovereignty rests with the people is the only practicable means of securing individual liberty.

IV

POLITICAL THOUGHT IN POETRY AFTER 1815

Consideration of the political thought in Shelley's poetry after 1815 brings us to his most famous works, and they are works of art rather than political doctrine. Only minor poems, and sometimes trivial ones, have a political theme. These will be considered at once. Much of the major poetry, however, reflects views on politics and reform, though it is never argumentative. An examination of this poetry will form the conclusion of this chapter.

Two sonnets, "To Wordsworth" and "Feelings of a Republican on the Fall of Bonaparte", published with *Alastor* in 1816, are expressions of regret. In the former Shelley deplores the apostasy to the liberal cause of such a powerful poet as Wordsworth. This idea is vehemently expressed in a letter to Peacock of July 25, 1818: "I wish you had sent me some of the overflowing villainy of those apostates [Southey and Wordsworth]. What a beastly and pitiful wretch that Wordsworth! That such a man should be such a poet!" [1]

"Feelings of a Republican on the Fall of Bonaparte" is an expression of regret that intense, constant passions of hatred and contempt were wasted upon Bonaparte. Though a spectacular enemy of the public good, he possessed only temporary and limited powers of evil. His fall reveals that the principal enemies of virtue were, and still are, "old Custom, Legal Crime, and bloody Faith". The somewhat banal poem, "Lines Written on

[1] *Julian Works*, vol. IX, p. 315. The letter was written apropos of an election in Westmorland in which the liberal candidate was narrowly defeated by a Tory. It was thought that support by Southey and Wordsworth for the conservative candidate contributed to the defeat. See White, *op. cit.*, vol. II, pp. 25-26.

Hearing the News of the Death of Napoleon", published in 1821, seems to imply a similar attitude. The earth turns, though Napoleon, a man of pomp and fierce strength, dies and in death is brought to nothing. The earth feeds upon the mighty, whom she fed.

The two poems on Napoleon reflect a belief that evils which can be identified with an individual are of necessity temporary and not of the first magnitude. Since tyrants are in a very real sense made by the people who submit to them, it is the people themselves who are the basic source of social evils.[2] Genuine amelioration must therefore come from slow, evolutionary changes in folk ways.

The series of poems in a popular style which Shelley wrote in the autumn of 1819 (see above, Chapter III, p. 46) were designed to be published "for the direct inspiration of the common people in the revolution that he thought was approaching".[3] They are "The Masque of Anarchy", "Lines Written during the Castlereagh Administration", "Song: To the Men of England", "Fragment: What Men Gain Fairly", "A New National Anthem", and "Sonnet: England in 1819". These poems, like almost all of the other political works, were posthumous publications.

[2] This idea is the theme of "Sonnet: Political Greatness" (written in 1820, published in 1824):
> Nor happiness, nor majesty, nor fame
> Nor peace, nor strength, nor skill in arms or arts,
> Shepherd those herds whom tyranny makes tame;
> . . . .
> What are numbers knit
> By force or custom? Man who man would be
> Must rule the empire of himself
> (*Cambridge Works*, p. 406).

[3] White, *op. cit.*, vol. II, p. 107. Though Shelley could hardly see any advantage to be gained from war, even when it is used for securing reform, he was prepared to take a stand if it should come. He wrote to Hunt on November 3, 1819 (*Julian Works*, vol. X, p. 119): "These ... are awful times. The tremendous question is now agitating, whether a military or a judicial despotism is to be established by our present rulers, or some form of government less unfavourable to the real and permanent interest of all men is to arise from the conflict of passions now gathering. We cannot hesitate which party to embrace; and whatever revolutions are to occur though oppression should change names and names cease to be oppressions, our party will be that of liberty and of the oppressed."

"Lines Written during the Castlereagh Administration" and "To Sidmouth and Castlereagh", first published in 1832, are invectives against the two government leaders (Sidmouth, the Home Secretary, and Castlereagh, the Foreign Secretary), whose policies, Shelley believed, were leading toward civil war. The sonnet "England in 1819", published in 1839, is a brief catalogue of the salient characteristics of the contemporary political picture. The invective in it matches that of the preceding poems. Featured in the picture are a king, who is "old, mad, blind, despised, and dying", "leech-like" rulers, a "starved and stabbed" people, a "liberticide" army, "golden and sanguine laws which tempt and slay", empty religion, and a senate, "Time's worst statute unrepealed", referring to the Roman Catholic disabilities. The conclusion is a note of Shelleyan optimism. Outmoded, these symbols of oppression and its work

> Are graves from which a glorious Phantom may
> Burst to illumine our tempestuous day.[4]

"Song: To the Men of England", first published in 1839, was designed to arouse the workers to resist the exploitation they suffered at the hands of the aristocracy. It follows a theme developed in *An Address to the People on the Death of the Princess Charlotte* (1817) and restated in *A Philosophical View of Reform* (1819): the products of laborers (the "Bees of England") become the possessions of the idle aristocracy (the "stingless drones") and thus increase their power; therefore the harder the workers work to produce, the more securely they forge their bonds.

"Fragment: To the People of England", published in 1862, emphasizes the dependence of the governing classes upon the hard-working poor, who are like gods to them, giving them all that they have. The other fragment, "What Men Gain Fairly", published in 1839, states in nine lines the idea presented in *A*

---

[4] Shelley used this imagery in 1817 as the conclusion of *An Address to the People on the Death of the Princess Charlotte* (*Shelley's Prose*, p. 169): "Let us follow the corpse of British Liberty slowly and reverentially to its tomb; and if some glorious Phantom should appear and make its throne of broken swords and sceptres and royal crowns trampled in the dust, let us say that the Spirit of Liberty has arisen from its grave."

Philosophical View of Reform on the ownership of property: claims to wealth gained from labor ("What men gain fairly") should be safeguarded, even though children of persons accumulating wealth in this way may live upon it in idleness ("Private injustice may be general good"). Those who gain wealth by "armed wrong", "guilty fraud" or "base compliances" deserve to be despoiled.

"The Masque of Anarchy", first published in 1832, is the longest of the political poems. Shelley wrote it in the autumn of 1819 after the "Peterloo Massacre" of August 16. The ugliness of the tyranny that is exhibited and denounced in the tracts is vividly imaged in this poem. Murder, Fraud, Hypocrisy (Castlereagh, Eldon, Sidmouth), and "many more Destructions" (bishops, lawyers, peers, spies) pass over England doing the bidding of Anarchy, their "God, and Law, and King". Fleeing before them is a "maniac maid", Hope, only surviving child of "weak and gray" Time. In despair she throws herself down in the street, expecting to be trampled by mounts of "Murder, Fraud, and Anarchy", but a "weak and frail" mist rises between her and her foes. It grows into a lofty, brilliant "Shape arrayed in mail" and passes "O'er the heads of men", leaving Anarchy and his followers dead. The Shape is the spirit of liberty. A voice as if from the indignant earth itself then cries out to the men of England:

> "Rise like lions after slumber
> In unvanquishable number,
> Shake your chains to earth like dew
> Which in sleep had fallen on you –
> Ye are many – they are few." [5]

The voice continues to describe the sources of England's grievances. They are the evils which were examined and condemned in the prose works. The industrious poor are kept in economic and political bondage to the idle aristocracy by

> "Paper coin – that forgery
> Of the title deeds." [6]

[5] *Cambridge Works*, p. 255.
[6] *Ibid.*

The resulting famine conditions are such as savage men and wild beasts have not known and would not endure. Freedom, on the other hand, would mean general welfare. It would be food, clothing, shelter, justice, wisdom, peace, love – the power to fight tyranny.

Finally the voice from the earth suggests a way of achieving freedom. It is the open assembly and passive resistance advocated in the pamphlets and tracts. The assembly should consist of all lovers of freedom – those from the "prison-halls of wealth and fashion" as well as those from the workhouse and prison. Together they should solemnly declare their freedom and meet the soldiers to disperse them by standing calm and resolute with folded arms.

In conclusion the voice repeats the stanza beginning, "Rise like lions after slumber." This injunction seems out of harmony with the principle of passive resistance, and Hunt's decision not to publish the poem was probably well advised.

Assembly in defiance of the law and passive resistance to the enforcers of the law are desperate means of securing freedom, but properly applied, they are effective. Thus the Indian masses under the leadership of Gandhi rendered their British rulers helpless in the 1930's. It is unlikely, however, that these methods could be applied with even partial success against an utterly ruthless government – a Hitler-like regime thriving upon deeds of depravity. Wholesale slaughter would be the result and harsh measures of reprisal adopted. The oppressed could hope to derive at best long range benefits. The attention of the outside world inevitably focuses upon such events, and sympathy for the victims rises. Public opinion thus tends to become united against the tyranny and to act in some measure as a deterrent. Though tyrants respect only force, a collective disapproval of their deeds tends to limit the spread of their power and puts them on the defensive.

"Liberty", written in 1820 but published posthumously in 1824, reflects the unleashed spirit of liberty as an elemental power operating upon mankind beside which upheavals in nature – storms and earthquakes – are puny. Shelley captures the startling, electric quality of this spirit in many of his important poems. He seems to have been able to feel it at work throughout the world.[7]

"Peter Bell the Third", written in October, 1819, but not published until 1839, is characterized by Shelley as a "party squib".[8] Though composed as a diversion, it has an undertone of seriousness. Peter Bell's dullness as a servant of the Devil is a lampoon of Wordsworth, whose decline in interest parallels his turning conservative. White observes,

> beneath the odd Shelleyan horseplay and occasional cutting parody, is plainly to be seen not only Shelley's warning that a poet who deserts the cause of freedom must necessarily grow dull, having committed a sort of spiritual suicide, but his very plain conviction that Wordsworth was already growing dull for this reason.[9]

This view is not out of harmony with that expressed in "Sonnet: To Wordsworth" (1816), the difference being that the sonnet laments Wordsworth's apostasy. "Peter Bell the Third" reflects no regret. It reveals the working of the principle that to forsake the ideals of liberty and to become an apologist for oppressive authority usher in a life of anti-climax and defeat.

Oedipus Tyrannus or Swellfoot the Tyrant was written in August, 1820, published without Shelley's name in December, and immediately suppressed under threat of prosecution after only seven copies had been sold. It is a political satire. Mary Shelley in a note describes it as "a plaything of the imagination" and observes that it "must not be judged for more than was meant".[10] Its indebtedness to contemporary cartoons and anony-

[7] Shelley was aware that he possessed this unique gift and describes it in a letter about *The Revolt of Islam*, dated December 11, 1817, to Godwin (*Julian Works*, vol. IX, p. 266): "I am formed, if for anything not in common with the herd of mankind, to apprehend minute and remote distinctions of feeling, whether relative to external nature or the living beings which surround us, and to communicate the conceptions which result from considering either the moral or the material universe as a whole."
[8] In a letter from Florence, dated November 2, 1819, Shelley writes to Leigh Hunt (*Julian Works*, vol. X, p. 104): "I have only expended a few days on this party squib and of course taken little pains. The verses and language I have let come as they would."
[9] White, *op. cit.*, vol. II, p. 169.
[10] *Cambridge Works*, p. 284.

mous political satires is pointed out by White and others.[11] Though the poem admittedly lacks importance and only partially succeeds as an attempt at humor, it reflects, as does "Peter Bell the Third", Shelley's serious views.

The form is that of a Greek drama in which swine (the inarticulate masses) make up the chorus. Among the more prominent members of the cast are Swellfoot (George IV), Iona Taurina (Queen Caroline), Mammon (Sidmouth), Purganax (Castlereagh), Dakry (Lord Eldon), and the Minotaur (John Bull).

The drama depicts the current English political scene, the focal point at the moment being the trial of Queen Caroline for infidelity. King Swellfoot orders the bothersome pigs that whine for want of grain slaughtered. To Purganax's forebodings over the mutiny of troops and the revenue failure, Mammon offers glib reassurances: "decimate some regiments", "come to my mint – coin paper". But the real source of Purganax's fear is the oracle, coined by Mammon in a moment of drunkenness (or inspiration):

"Boeotia, choose reform or civil war,
When through thy streets, instead of hare with dogs,
A Consort-Queen shall hunt a King with hogs,
Riding on the Ionian Minotaur." [12]

A Leech, a Gadfly, and a Rat have been sent to torment Iona, who is abroad, and prevent her from returning to fulfill the prophecy. Mammon, lacking faith in the oracle, fears the Swine, who "boast their descent / From the Minotaur". All efforts to prevent Iona's return are in vain. Upon arrival, she gains the following of the Swine, who shout, "Long live Iona! down with Swellfoot!" Mammon then produces the Green Bag filled with the concentrated poison of slander and sealed with the seal of Fraud. The Bag's contents when poured on any subject will turn innocence to guilt, but the Pigs must be made to believe that they will prove innocence as well as guilt. Thus it may be pretended that the Bag will serve as a fair test of Iona's innocence or guilt. Mammon, claiming to act in the interest of clearing Iona's good name, which rumors have besmirched, will then administer the

[11] See White, *op. cit.*, vol. II, pp. 224-226.
[12] *Cambridge Works*, p. 286.

contents and thereby discredit her. This scheme is to be worked in a ceremony which is to be held at a feast honoring the goddess Famine. Painstaking preparations put everything in readiness, and the show begins. As it is being enacted in the Temple of Famine, the figure of Liberty appears, proclaims Famine her eternal foe, and commands her to rise. At this moment as Swellfoot and his ministers are ready to empty the contents of the Bag upon Iona's head, Iona snatches the Bag and empties it upon them, whereupon Swellfoot and his whole court are turned into ugly beasts. The image of Famine sinks through the floor, and the Minotaur emerges. Iona mounts upon his back and exits, driving the Swine in pursuit of the beasts.

Shelley was not the enthusiastic champion of Queen Caroline that he seems to be in *Swellfoot the Tyrant*. Nevertheless, he aligns himself with the Queen because of her opposition to George IV and his ministers.[13] Employing stock symbols of contemporary pamphleteer literature and cartoons, he puts into *Swellfoot* the views he developed in the prose tracts and expresses in letters. England must come to reform or civil war. Swellfoot and his ministers display the contempt of the aristocracy for the suffering masses, and the corrupt practices which were employed to maintain dictatorial power. Use of spies by the government, failure of the courts to administer justice, growing taxes upon the poor (used to swell pensions and patronage, and to deprive the workers of the produce of their land), the printing of paper money, the savage repression of the growing restiveness among the people – all of these evils with which Shelley comes to grips in the tracts are shown in this drama, whose plot depicts England moving to the brink of revolution. Though lacking original imagery and merit as a poem, the work is significant as a graphic picture of Shelley's political views.

"An Ode Written in October, 1819, Before the Spaniards Had

[13] White writes (*op. cit.*, vol. II, p. 225), "Shelley ... thought the charges [against Queen Caroline] probably exaggerated. His principal feeling ... was one of disgust that 'a vulgar cook-maid' should somehow become a symbol in the fight against oppression. Nevertheless, her enemies were worse than she, and were also enemies of Freedom. Though he scorned her, he was technically on her side."

Recovered Their Liberty", published with *Prometheus Unbound* in 1820, is another product of the political excitement which was intensified in Shelley by events in England and on the Continent. Written in an ardent missionary style, this poem conjures the Spanish people, enslaved by state and church, to awaken, arise, resist. It celebrates the true patriots who have fought, suffered greatly, and met with defeat; typically Shelleyan, it anticipates the victory that will have been gained when the people shake off their chains. The underlying idea, expressed in the line "The slave and the tyrant are twin-born foes", is a recurring theme in Shelley's political works. The people's acceptance of bondage creates twin enemies, the tyrant and the slave.

"Ode to Liberty", inspired by the revolution in Spain, was written in the spring of 1820 and published with *Prometheus Unbound*. In exalted, visionary imagery this poem surveys much the same ground as does the analytical *Philosophical View of Reform*, which was being written at about the same time. Its theme is the history and power (both the demonstrated and the potential) of freedom.

Carried by the electric spirit of liberty generated in Spain, Shelley attains a panoramic view of the world as it was and is. Before the advent of liberty "this divinest universe / Was yet a chaos and a curse". The eat-or-be-eaten law of the jungle was kindled and prevailed. Ancient societies, built by their rulers upon slavery and blood, emerged with the growing population, which "Was savage, cunning, blind, and rude".

The spirit of liberty first appeared in Greece, bringing with it the immortal works of the Athenian civilization. Rome, nourished by it, became great only to sink into tyranny. Liberty then disappeared from view for a thousand years. The reign of Alfred the Great marked its return. Citadels of liberty sprang up in Italy. Luther, catching and reflecting its spirit, awakened nations from trance-like medieval slumber. In England it was the impulse which guided the prophets of the Renaissance and produced immortal art. Though withdrawn from the scene, it enabled Milton to see beyond his own dark days. The light of freedom again split the gloom of oppression with such startling brilliance that men were staggered "with a glad surprise". This was the French Revolution. Following the excesses of violence Napoleon rose to darken the world again. His fate, like that of other tyrants, now haunts all "victor kings in their ancestral towers".

Viewing the present, Shelley finds that "England yet sleeps ... Spain calls her now". Compared to the "links of steel" which the heroic Spanish people have broken, England's bonds are mere "threads of gold". The spirit of the German hero Arminius still lives in "King-deluded Germany". Let Italy, worshiping past glories, repress her bestial rulers. King and priest are words which camouflage the evils they represent. Let the brilliance of free minds illuminate such words and strip them of their obscurity. Man, "crowned ... the King of Life", sacrifices his capacity to conquer when he willfully enthrones oppression and oppressor. Let liberty bring wisdom out of man's deep spirit, for do not liberty and wisdom come to judge truthfully "life's ill-apportioned lot?" If liberty and liberty's adjuncts – justice, fame, and hope – could be purchased with tears and blood, have not the wise and free already bought them? The vision fades.

"Ode to Liberty" is a poetic affirmation of some of the political concepts analyzed in *A Philosophical View of Reform*. History shows that freedom pervades the heights of man's attainments. The death of freedom has inevitably brought a decline in human welfare. The spirit of liberty is invoked as the great, irrepressible civilizing force of the world. Man is enslaved only when he is willing to be.

"Ode to Naples", written in August, 1820, and published posthumously in 1824,[14] hails Naples, which had just won a constitutional government, as the "signal and the seal" of the hopes of all Italy for reform. The triumph of the Neapolitans, though short-lived, was part of the contemporary European revolutionary movement that elated Shelley. The poem anticipates the Austrian counterattack which ended Naples' newly won

---

[14] According to White, *op. cit.*, vol. II, p. 223, on October 1 and 8 the poem appeared without Shelley's permission in "*The Military Register and Weekly Gazette, Historical, Literary*, etc. *for the Army, Navy, Colonies, and Fashionable World*, edited and published by R. Scott, 3 Pall Mall Court."

freedom in 1821 ("The Anarchs of the North lead forth their legions / Like Chaos o'er creation, uncreating"), but poignantly invokes the spirit of love and beauty to protect and preserve the freedom of the city.

"Ode to Naples" and the other minor poems with political themes which were written after 1815 reflect various aspects of Shelley's thought. The sonnet "To Wordsworth" (1816) is a rebuke to an apostate from liberalism. "Feelings of a Republican on the Fall of Bonaparte" (1816) and "Lines Written on Hearing the News of the Death of Napoleon" (1821) point by implication to the importance of social amelioration through "a slow, gradual, silent change".[15] Poems such as "England in 1819" and "Lines Written During the Castlereagh Administration" are invectives against the government's leaders and deeds. "The Masque of Anarchy" balances against a picture of tyranny in England in 1819 the image of the eventually triumphal spirit of liberty. "Ode to Liberty" (1820) concludes with a trumpet call to the oppressed in England and on the Continent to awaken to their responsibility for reform. These poems share one characteristic: they are enthusiastically didactic in the *Queen Mab* vein. Major poems of political significance, which were written during the same period, hold to objective artistic standards while obeying a didactic impulse.

The major poems that more clearly represent Shelley's political thought are *The Revolt of Islam, Prometheus Unbound*, and *Hellas*. Being narrative, they are portrayals in which political truths may be discerned. They belong to the class of reform poetry but avoid moralizing. In the Preface to *The Revolt of Islam* (1817) Shelley indicates his intention to follow objective standards of poetic art in the creation of the poem without abandoning his design to spread the ideals of reform:

I have made no attempt to recommend the motives which I would

---

[15] The phrase occurs in the Preface to *The Revolt of Islam* (1817) and is part of Shelley's expression of confidence in the evolutionary social progress of the human race (*Cambridge Works*, p. 46): "mankind appear to me to be emerging from their trance. I am aware, me thinks, of a slow, gradual, silent change."

substitute for those at present governing mankind, by methodical and systematic argument. I would only awaken the feelings, so that the reader should see the beauty of true virtue, and be incited to those inquiries which have led to my moral and political creed, and that of some of the sublimest intellects in the world. The Poem therefore (with the exception of the first Canto, which is purely introductory) is narrative, not didactic.[16]

That Shelley by 1817 came to condemn didacticism in poetry [17] while adhering to the reform motive seems paradoxical. It is in fact evidence of his perception that great works of art exercise a moral power far exceeding that of exhortation.[18] His major poems from this time on were therefore designed as portrayals that would shadow forth human truths. Their appeal would be to arouse in readers a sympathy for the principles they embody. Poems written according to this technique evince what has been called Shelley's "myth-making faculty".

The Revolt of Islam (known originally as *Laon and Cythna*) was composed in 1817 in "little more than six months".[19] It depicts a revolution that is "the *beau ideal* ... of the French Revolution" [20] and is written in the Spenserian stanza. Biographical data gathered from Mary Shelley's journal show that Shelley was reading *The Faerie Queene* aloud and a history of

---

[16] *Cambridge Works*, p. 45. In a letter of September 24, 1817, to Byron concerning the poem Shelley says (*Julian Works*, vol. IX, p. 246), "It is in the style and for the same object as 'Queen Mab', but interwoven with a story of human passion."
[17] His best known statement of this opinion appears in the Preface to *Prometheus Unbound* (*Cambridge Works*, p. 164): "Didactic poetry is my abhorrence; nothing can be equally well expressed in prose that is not tedious and supererogatory in verse." Even while composing his masterpiece in 1819 he could, as we have seen, be moved to write "The Masque of Anarchy" and later (1820) the exalted, visionary "Ode to Liberty".
[18] *A Defence of Poetry*, written in 1821, asserts that "Poets are the unacknowledged legislators of the world" (*Shelley's Prose*, p. 297).
[19] Preface to *The Revolt of Islam, Cambridge Works*, p. 48. Thomas Medwin in *The Life of Percy Bysshe Shelley* (A New Edition, 1913), pp. 178-179, says, "Shelley told me that he and Keats had mutually agreed, in the same given time, (six months each,) to write a long poem, and that *Endymion*, and *Revolt of Islam* were the fruits of this rivalry."
[20] Shelley's letter of October 13, 1817, to a publisher, *Julian Works*, vol. IX, p. 251.

the French Revolution during various of the stages of composition.[21] It is his longest, though far from best, poem.

Published in 1818 after undergoing revisions late in 1817 which included a change in title, *The Revolt of Islam* was designed as "an experiment on the temper of the public mind as to how far a thirst for a happier condition of moral and political society survives among the enlightened and refined, the tempests which have shaken the age in which we live".[22] It was also an experiment in the "myth-making" technique of communication:

> I have sought to enlist the harmony of metrical language, the ethereal combinations of the fancy, the rapid and subtle transitions of human passion, all those elements which essentially compose a poem, in the cause of a liberal and comprehensive morality; and in the view of kindling within the bosoms of my readers a virtuous enthusiasm for those doctrines of liberty and justice, that faith and hope in something good, which neither violence, nor misrepresentation, nor prejudice, can ever totally extinguish among mankind.[23]

The Preface contains a catalogue of ideas which the poem is designed to exemplify. It is, by and large, a list of the principles expressed in the early tracts: "the bloodless dethronement of ... oppressors"; "the unveiling of the religious frauds by which ... [the people] had been deluded into submission"; "the tranquility of successful patriotism"; "the universal toleration and benevolence of true philanthropy"; "the treachery and barbarity of hired soldiers"; "the consequences of legitimate despotism, – civil war, famine, plague, superstition, and an utter extinction of the domestic affections"; "the temporary triumph of oppression, that secure earnest of its final and inevitable fall".[24]

The defects of the poem – faulty structure, obscurity, repetitious description, sentimentality – that make it no more popular today than it was when it first appeared,[25] need not conceal the

---

[21] White, *op. cit.*, vol. I, p. 527.
[22] Preface to *The Revolt of Islam, Cambridge Works*, p. 45.
[23] *Ibid.*
[24] *Ibid.*
[25] Byron, in a letter to John Murray, dated November 24, 1818, says, "[A review attacking Shelley in the *Quarterly Review*] has *sold* an edition of the *Revolt of Islam*, which, otherwise, nobody would have thought of reading, and few who read can understand – I for one" (*The Works of*

political ideas it embodies or the method of their representation. The framework poem (Canto I and Canto XII, stanzas xvii-xli), in which the story of Laon and Cythna – "a story of human passion in its most universal character" [26] – is placed, is a myth. In it the eternal struggle between good and evil is symbolized by the fight between the Serpent and the Eagle, and the Temple of the Spirit of Good is pictured. The youth who tells the story is driven by "visions of despair" (Canto I, stanza i), brought on by contemplation of the failure of the French Revolution, to the place where he witnesses the defeat of the Serpent (Good) by the Eagle (Evil). He is told that the battle will be renewed, that the victor has most to fear at the moment when his victory is complete because this moment generates the forces which will inevitably bring about his downfall. In the Temple of the Spirit of Good, where the symbol of Good changes from Serpent to radiant male Form, the youth is instructed to listen to "A tale of human power" (Canto I, stanza lviii) and to learn. The tale he hears is that of Laon and Cythna, whose forms become visible. It is an account of how their lives were spent in promoting the ideal revolution and of how the revolution was crushed. The last twenty-five stanzas of the poem (Canto XII, stanzas xvii-xli), in which Laon and Cythna are brought after death to the Temple where we find them in Canto I, complete the framework.

The framework poem, which provides a cosmic setting for the telling of the human story, reflects Shelley's belief in the inevitability of political progress. The war between the Snake and the Eagle, which shakes the world's foundations, occurs whenever "mankind doth strive / With its oppressors in a strife of blood", or whenever "free thoughts, like lightnings, are alive, / And in each bosom of the multitude / Justice and Truth with custom's hydra brood / Wage silent war", or whenever "priests and kings dissemble / In smiles or frowns their fierce disquietude", or whenever "round pure hearts a host of hopes assemble" (Canto I, stanza xxxiii). The undying impulse for reform is the spirit of the

---

Lord Byron: Letters and Journals, edited by Rowland E. Prothero, vol. IV, p. 273).
[26] Preface to *The Revolt of Islam, Cambridge Works*, p. 45.

individual, which is always beyond being completely controlled by oppressors.

The human story, related by Laon, is intended to illustrate the reform principles at work. Laon, a reflective youth of contemporary Greece [27] which has fallen victim to despotism, has heard "life's various story, / And in no careless heart transcribed the tale" (Canto II, stanza ix). The heritage of Greece had been betrayed by "Feeble historians", "False disputants", "Victims who worshipped ruin", and "slaves who loathed their state, / Yet ... [flattered] Power" (Canto II, stanza iii). The people sought "All that despair from murdered hope inherits ... and, in their helpless misery blind, / A deeper prison and heavier chains did find, / And stronger tyrants" (Canto II, stanza vi). The ultimate source of the bondage which produces misery throughout the social order is man's will:

> For they all pined in bondage; body and soul,
> Tyrant and slave, victim and torturer, bent
> Before one Power, to which supreme control
> Over their will by their own weakness lent
> Made all its many names omnipotent;
> All symbols of things evil, all divine
> (Canto II, stanza viii).

These lines, incidentally, reflect Shelley's belief that in a society made up of a ruling class and a serving class, the rulers are as much bound to unhappy social and political conditions as are the masses.

Fate has put Laon in the unhappy land, "a dungeon to my blasted kind" (Canto II, stanza vi), to search for a kindred spirit. An orphan, the fair Cythna, who has been cared for by Laon's parents, acquires a sympathy for his love of wisdom and truth, and hatred of oppression – feelings which have been strengthened in him by study of the works of the Greek immortals. Sharing ideals, Laon and Cythna look forward to a joint crusade against

[27] Shelley comments upon the setting of the story of Laon and Cythna in the letter to a publisher (October 12, 1817) cited above (Footnote #20, p. 79): "The scene is supposed to be laid in Constantinople and modern Greece, but without much attempt at minute delineation of Mahometan manners."

tyranny. Cythna will champion political equality for women ("'Can man be free if woman be a slave?'" (Canto II, stanza xliii)).

After being captured and placed in chains in prison by slaves of the Tyrant who carry Cythna to the Golden City, Laon suffers a period of madness. As his senses are partly restored, he becomes aware that an old man, whose "sweet and mighty eloquence" (Canto IV, stanza xi) had caused the guards to open the prison, is transporting him in a sailboat to a peaceful harbor. The old man ("That gentle Hermit" (Canto IV, stanza v)) brings Laon to his secluded, sylvan home and tends him with soothing words and kindness until his health is restored.

The Hermit tells Laon that among the people

> Kind thoughts, and mighty hopes, and gentle deeds
> Abound; for fearless love, and the pure law
> Of mild equality and peace, succeeds
> To faiths which long have held the world in awe,
> Bloody, and false, and cold
> (Canto IV, stanza xv).

These new ideas and attitudes of the people hold promise that bloodless revolution may be achieved through the strength of words. A maiden, whose "quiet words" secured her release from torturers (Canto IV, stanzas xviii-xix), goes about teaching a doctrine of equal laws and justice for women that may bring about the overthrow of tyrants without war.

Laon, strengthened by the Hermit's story, travels far to the City of Gold (Constantinople), where he hopes to find that the maiden is Cythna. Arriving in the night at the Camp of the revolutionists (patriots), situated outside of the City, he discovers that "now the Power of Good ... [holds] victory" (Canto V, stanza ii). As he chats with a youthful guard ("the youth / In whom its earliest hopes my spirit found" (Canto V, stanza v)), "a sound of sweeping conflict" (Canto V, stanza vi) arouses the sleeping revolutionists. All hurry toward the sound and upon arriving at its source find that enemy soldiers have attacked and slain ten thousand patriots as they slept. The enemy forces flee in confusion upon hearing someone cry, "Laon!" They are pursued and brought to bay, whereupon "revenge and fear / Made the high virtue of the patriots fail" (Canto V, stanza viii). A patriot strikes at one of the enemy with his spear, but Laon intervenes and receives the thrust. This act cools the passions of the patriot and restores in him the spirit of love for mankind from which the revolution derives its power and success. Laon, though wounded, explains to the enemy soldiers that they have slain men whose only mission was to bestow upon them "truth's freedom" (Canto V, stanza x). His speech reconciles the opposing forces, and together they joyfully go toward the City:

> Lifting the thunder of their acclamation,
> Towards the City then the multitude,
> And I among them, went in joy – a nation
> Made free by love; a mighty brotherhood
> Linked by a jealous interchange of good
> (Canto V, stanza xiv).

This incident is a representation of ideas expressed as early as 1812 in *An Address to the Irish People*. Concerning the principle of nonviolence as a method of promoting the successful revolution (see above, Chapter II, p. 32), Shelley wrote in the *Address*:

I agree with the Quakers so far as they disclaim violence and trust their cause wholly and solely to its own truth. ... In no case employ violence; the way of liberty and happiness is never to transgress the rules of virtue and justice. ... If you can descend to use the same weapons as your enemy, you put yourself on a level with him on this score; you must be convinced that he is on these grounds your superior.

. . . .

Wherever has violence succeeded? The French Revolution, although undertaken with the best intentions, ended ill for the people, because violence was employed. The cause which they vindicated was that of truth, but they gave it the appearance of a lie by using methods which will suit the purposes of liars as well as their own.[28]

The incident also serves as a commentary upon Shelley's faith that constant, consistent appeals to reason (supported by good will and courageous action) will promote a universal brotherhood which, in turn, will eliminate social and political evils. The

---

[28] *Shelley's Prose*, pp. 46-47.

patriots are ready to indulge their passion for revenge when Laon, acting as their leader, controls it by intervening. After he has received a wound intended for an enemy, his words on brotherhood become convincing because they have been supported by courageous, unselfish action.

There is no suggestion in this episode that human passions have disappeared or will disappear. What is suggested is that an enlightened, unselfish leadership can act in such a way as to control them before their destructive force is set in motion. There is the suggestion also that a generous act toward an adversary will carry more influence with him than a display of strength. Viewed artistically, this incident is sentimental utopianism, but the principle which it embodies has viability.

In the next episode the scene shifts to the City. Laon and the reconciled forces arrive to find the citizenry celebrating their newly won freedom. The fallen Tyrant (Othman) sits in the Imperial House "Upon the footstool of his golden throne" (Canto V, stanza xx). He had been deserted by everyone except a frail but beautiful child. As Laon leads Othman and the child out of the palace, an angry crowd gathers and demands that justice be done:

> "He who judged, let him be brought
> To judgment! blood for blood cries from the soil
> On which his crimes have deep pollution wrought!"
> (Canto V, stanza xxxii).

Laon saves Othman's life by addressing the crowd:

> "What do ye seek? what fear ye ... that
> ye should shed
> The blood of Othman? – if your hearts are tried
> In the true love of freedom, cease to dread
> This one poor lonely man –
>
> . . . .
> let him go free; until the worth
> Of human nature win ... a second birth"
> (Canto V, stanza xxxiii).

The speech closes with the observation that " 'The chastened will / Of virtue sees that justice is the light / Of love, and not revenge and terror and despite' " (Canto V, stanza xxxiv). Laon's words subdue the people as they subdued the revenge-minded army earlier. Appeals to reason continue to promote the good will among men which governs the revolution.

On the following day Laon discovers that Laone, the leader of the bloodless revolution, is Cythna and that the doctrine of equal rights for women is a principal motivating force of the revolution. Happily reunited, Laon and Cythna come to the gate of the City after a day-long festival. At the moment of their arrival the allies of Othman attack. In the ensuing confusion Laon and Cythna are separated. Great numbers of the patriots are slaughtered. Amid the bloody chaos Laon rallies the revolutionists "with cries of scorn" (Canto VI, stanza viii) for their panic and fear of death. A few of them join Laon, and together they passively resist the invaders. This desperate maneuver fills the invading army with doubt even in victory, but as the battle intensifies, all of Laon's companions are slain. As he prepares to meet the fate of his comrades, he is rescued by Cythna, who rides through the ranks of the foe on "A black Tartarian horse of giant frame" whose "path ... [makes] a solitude" (Canto VI, stanzas xix-xx).

The revolution is crushed by the allies of Othman. The remainder of the poem gives an account of Cythna's life following her capture by the slaves of the Tyrant and describes the execution of a plot by Othman's Priests to sacrifice Laon and Cythna upon a "pyre of expiation" (Canto X, stanza xxxviii) to Heaven because the City is held in the grip of Plague and Famine. In conclusion, Laon and Cythna are transported after death to the Temple of the Spirit of Good, where they appear at the beginning of the poem.

The utopianism of *The Revolt of Islam* largely obscures the useful political doctrine of the poem. The revolution of the Golden City, as White observes, "is brought about largely by the fact that both Laon and Cythna are freed by the tyrants to preach revolution. They go free through no compulsion except the power of persuasion".[29] The practical aspects of revolution are not pictured. Food and shelter for the population are not a problem.

[29] White, *op. cit.*, vol. I, p. 532.

The days are filled with joyous celebrations. Hard work has no place in the new regime.

The poem, however, does embody tenets of Shelley's political faith, as we have seen. The promise of lasting political reform is to be found in humanity's ability to subdue passions of hatred, revenge, and prejudice. Reasonable arguments charged with good will and the spirit of brotherhood will produce reasonable behavior. Good will and the spirit of brotherhood will reproduce themselves. Non-violent opposition even at the price of annihilation is the proper response to force of arms. Mankind's knowledge of these means is assurance that reform will ultimately come. The overthrow of the revolution in *The Revolt*, therefore, does not warrant pessimism because it is of no real consequence.

Prometheus Unbound, begun in the fall of 1818 and completed during the winter of 1819-1820, was published "probably in August [1820]".[30] It is almost universally recognized as Shelley's masterpiece.[31] Its value, like that of other great poems, is infinite. The large and growing mass of scholarly comment upon the intense drama, the unmatched lyric beauty, the highly original imagery, and the allegory of the poem is evidence of its appeal and challenge to reflective readers.

Shelley says in the Preface that he intended to do more than "restore the lost drama of Aeschylus". His *Prometheus Unbound* is an adaptation of the Greek myth. After describing and justifying the changes he had made in the Aeschylean story, he concludes, "Prometheus is, as it were, the type of the highest perfection of moral and intellectual nature impelled by the purest and truest

---

[30] White, *op. cit.*, vol. II, p. 138.
[31] Shelley was a good judge of his own works. In a letter to Charles and James Ollier, dated Oct. 15, 1819, he says (*Julian Works*, vol. X, p. 95), "[*Prometheus Unbound*] is the most perfect of my productions." Again in writing to Charles Ollier on December 15 [or 25], 1819, he says (*ibid.*, vol. X, p. 135), "My 'Prometheus Unbound' is the best thing I ever wrote." Though he later refers to *Adonais* as "perhaps the least imperfect of my compositions" (Shelley to Charles Ollier, June 11, 1821, *ibid.*, vol. X, p. 275), the *Prometheus Unbound* almost perfectly fulfills the high standards and purposes of poetry as he conceived of them. He was aware, however, that the imaginative originality of the poem would prevent it from selling: "I think, if I may judge by its merits, the 'Prometheus' cannot sell beyond

motives to the best and noblest ends." [32] This observation serves as a guide to an interpretation of the poem. The drama is intended to shed light upon the best qualities of human nature. It treats of moral principles, which, when translated into political terms, relate primarily to the psychology of individual self-government rather than to social government. Consequently, we should not expect to find, and in fact do not find, that the poem is a direct commentary upon specific problems of political reform. It is, rather, a dramatic account of reform of self and the consequences of such reform.

The orthodox interpretation of the poem, representing the consensus of scholarly opinion, makes Prometheus the symbol of the mind of man. Hence, the action of the play – the struggle between Prometheus and his captor, Jupiter, the torture of Prometheus by the Furies, the overthrow of Jupiter by Demogorgon, the release of Prometheus by Hercules, the reunion of Prometheus and Asia – represents mental bondage, mental agony, and mental liberation and triumph. Jupiter, deriving his power from the mind he enslaves, becomes hatred and despair within the mind. Jupiter's agents, the Furies ("We are the ministers of pain, and fear, / And disappointment, and mistrust, and hate, / And clinging crime" (Act I, 11. 452-454)), are forms of mental torture. Prometheus's recall of his curse against Jupiter is a mental or psychological revolution. It makes possible the arrival of the hour of Jupiter's overthrow by Demogorgon (Necessity), who is Jupiter's child ("Detested prodigy" (Act III, Scene i, 1. 61)). Hercules (Strength, minister "To wisdom, courage, and long-suffering love" (Act III, Scene iii, 1. 1), unchains Prometheus, and Prometheus is reunited with Asia (Love). The reunion is therefore the result of a series of events set in motion by the moral reformation of an individual.

A political interpretation has been advanced by Professor Cameron.[33] It is his purpose "to make a consistent interpretation

---

twenty copies" (Shelley to Charles and James Ollier, March 6, 1820, *ibid.*, vol. X, p. 148).
[32] Preface to *Prometheus Unbound, Cambridge Works*, p. 163.
[33] K. N. Cameron, "The Political Symbolism of *Prometheus Unbound*",

of ... [*Prometheus Unbound*] in terms of [a certain political-historical content]".[34] He asserts that "The concept of Prometheus as the intellectuals, the intelligentsia, is inherent in Aeschylus's picture of him as inventor of all arts and sciences." [35] Consequently, Shelley's Prometheus symbolizes the intellectuals of the day who understand the need for political reform in England and on the Continent. Cameron observes that this interpretation of Prometheus "fits in very nicely with Shelley's own special theory of the 'Poets', those 'unacknowledged legislators of the world', who have made possible all human progress".[36]

The Furies "represent not only the crimes of the Napoleonic Wars; they represent all the satellites and agents of court and state by means of which – as well as by its armies – the ruling aristocratic class kept itself in power".[37] Cameron adds, "This interpretation does not, of course, rule out other interpretations. ... The Furies represent, also, in a general ethical sense, tormenting thoughts of all kinds oppressing man." [38]

The traditional interpretations of Asia as Love and Demogorgon as Necessity are retained. Cameron feels, however, that the idea of Demogorgon as Necessity or Fate cannot adequately suggest the "political-historical" meaning Shelley intended to convey. He says,

[Demogorgon] is not only Necessity or Fate in a general sense but Necessity in the special, semi-scientific sense given to the concept by Godwin and Hume. ... Not only is the physical world subject to these blind and immutable forces; the world of human society, human history, is governed by them also. In the contemporary historical situation, these forces were, Shelley believed, inexorably working for the overthrow of the old order and the establishment of a new.[39]

PMLA (Publications of the Modern Language Association of America), vol. LVIII (September, 1943), pp. 728-753.
[34] *Ibid.*, p. 728.
[35] *Ibid.*, p. 733.
[36] *Ibid.*
[37] *Ibid.*, p. 731. Cameron rests this interpretation primarily upon similarities between passages representing the Furies in *Prometheus Unbound* and those inspired by the Napoleonic wars in *The Revolt of Islam*.
[38] *Ibid.*, p. 732.
[39] *Ibid.*, p. 742.

In the specific historical situation of ... [Shelley's] own age the powers of Necessity were making for an overthrow of the existing social order, but if those powers acted without the aid of the spirit of love and brotherhood all their efforts would be in vain and a new despotism would arise. Demogorgon can overthrow the old order without the aid of Asia, but he cannot build a new one unless she assists him.[40]

Cameron agrees with those who interpret Jupiter as tyranny but believes that "In terms of political allegory ... as distinguished from the general social allegory, he represents not just tyranny but the tyrannical rule of Metternich, Castlereagh, and their satellites, and tyranny of the Holy Alliance, to the overthrow of which Shelley looked forward." [41]

Thetis, wife of Jupiter, "represents the false hopes of the despots for the perpetuation of their rule".[42] This view is derived from Jupiter's belief that Thetis will help to make his rule eternal, whereas "she is not really eternity, only 'that bright image of eternity' which, according to Plato, is 'time' ".[43] As such she represents the temporal limits of Jupiter's reign.

Cameron's political interpretation is intriguing. The persons and events of the contemporary political scene with which characters and action in *Prometheus Unbound* are identified were very much in Shelley's mind as he composed his masterpiece. They are discussed in letters and prose works, as we have seen. Revolution is hailed in three short poems, "An Ode Written in October, 1819, Before the Spaniards Had Recovered Their Liberty", "Ode to Liberty" (1820), and "Ode to Naples" (1820). But to see *Prometheus Unbound* primarily as a reflection of historical persons and events is to surrender the universal quality of the myth in the poem. It is to overlook Shelley's extraordinary skill at dramatizing the abstract [44] and to disregard his prefatory

[40] *Ibid.*, p. 744.
[41] *Ibid.*, p. 748.
[42] *Ibid.*
[43] *Ibid.*
[44] Shelley reluctantly resolved to exercise this talent at the end of his Irish venture in 1812 (see above, Chapter II, p. 27): "I will look to events in which it will be impossible that I can share. ... Wholly to abstract our views from self, undoubtedly requires unparalleled disinterestedness. There is not a completer abstraction than labouring for distant ages."

description of Prometheus as "the type of the highest perfection of moral and intellectual nature impelled by the purest and the truest motives to the best and noblest ends". Shelley was capable of analyzing contemporary political problems in *A Philosophical View of Reform* and of symbolizing moral and psychological truths in *Prometheus Unbound* simultaneously.

The basic objection that may be raised against Cameron's interpretation is that often he must shift his ground when interpreting the action of the drama. For example, after identifying the Furies as "the armies of the Napoleonic Wars . . . [and] all the satellites and agents of court and state", he states that they "represent, also, in a general ethical sense, tormenting thoughts of all kinds oppressing man". This change permits an explanation of the Furies' torture of Prometheus that resembles the orthodox interpretation: "the intellectuals of . . . [Shelley's] own day . . . [are] tormented by thoughts of a Europe devastated by a quarter of a century of wars and oppression apparently never to rise again".[45] The meaning of the Furies must be broadened in this way if the allegory of the scene is to be made intelligible. Prometheus (the intellectuals who saw the necessity of reform) could not be represented as suffering physical torture at the hands of "the armies of the Napoleonic Wars . . . [and] all the satellites and agents of court and state".

Professor Carlos Baker's examination of Cameron's interpretation supplies a detailed account of the difficulties of applying particularized meanings to the action of the play.[46] Baker concludes,

It is everywhere evident that in order to apply his social-group symbols to the interpretation of the play, . . . [Cameron] must in effect abandon them, or translate them into mind-symbols which in effect refute the social-group symbols. Insofar as he does so, he is undoubtedly moving in the right direction; but to the extent that he moves in the right direction he abandons his initial assumptions. That is, he abandons the specific socio-political context (in terms of which

---

[45] Cameron, "The Political Symbolism of *Prometheus Unbound*", op. cit., p. 733.
[46] See Carlos Baker, *Shelley's Major Poetry*, Appendix III, "The Political and Scientific Interpretations of *Prometheus Unbound*", pp. 283-285.

he wishes to view the play) in favor of a broader ethical context which is only tangentially related to the particularized meanings he alleges.[47]

The important ideas embodied in *Prometheus Unbound* emerge only when its ethical and psychological implications are considered. It is a dramatic account of reform of the individual which exposes the moral foundations of political reform. The moral principles by which the individual governs or disciplines himself serve as the beginning point and a point of reference for political reform. Shelley advanced this doctrine in *An Address to the Irish People* (1812). His comments upon governmental practices in *A Philosophical View of Reform* (1820) show that he does not now envisage individual morality, lofty and universal though it might be, as a replacement for political organization and the work of making political institutions function. Laws which promote both the physical and psychical welfare of each member of society within a given state are based upon, and grow out of high individualistic ideals, but they must be formulated and tested in practice. They do not formulate themselves or appear spontaneously. Since *Prometheus Unbound* is primarily a moral allegory dramatizing revolution of the human spirit, it constitutes an attack upon the problem of evil. Man's will to reform becomes the agent for eradication of evil. No outside power is needed. This moral doctrine of the poem stands in relationship to the political doctrine of *A Philosophical View of Reform* as constitutional law does to statutory law. The former deals with ethical principles that seem to be rooted in human nature, the latter with political doctrine which is dictated by them.

Hellas, written in the fall of 1821 and published "in the spring (probably March) of 1822",[48] is the last of Shelley's major political poems. Shelley says in the Preface that the poem is designed to celebrate the Greek struggle for independence and is modeled upon the *Persae* of Aeschylus. He adds,

the decision of the glorious contest now waging in Greece being yet suspended forbids a catastrophe parallel to the return of Xerxes and

[47] Baker, *op. cit.*, p. 285.
[48] White, *op. cit.*, vol. II, p. 330.

the desolations of the Persians. I have, therefore, contended myself with exhibiting a series of lyric pictures and with having wrought upon the curtain of futurity, which falls upon the unfinished scene, such figures of indistinct and visionary delineation as suggest the final triumph of the Greek cause as a portion of the cause of civilization and social improvement.[49]

This is an accurate description of the poem. It shows that *Hellas* belongs to the group of political works which includes "An Ode Written in October, 1819, Before the Spaniards Had Recovered Their Liberty", "Ode to Liberty", and "Ode to Naples". Like these poems it acclaims an event of the contemporary revolutionary movement, but it is also akin to *The Revolt of Islam* and *Prometheus Unbound* in form and content. Despite the thinness of plot it is a drama envisioning the emergence of a new "great age" ("The world's great age begins anew" (1. 1060)) against a background of ignorance, brutality, and the clash of armies. As with the failure of the revolution in *The Revolt of Islam*, so with *Hellas* the possible failure of the Greek revolution is of little significance as long as the forces of liberty remain alive. They become most dynamic when their suppression is most complete. This is also the central idea of Demogorgon's concluding speech in *Prometheus Unbound*.

The opening scene of *Hellas* finds Mahmud, Sultan of Turkey, in a troubled sleep. He awakens from disturbing dreams with the foreboding sense that stormy times lie ahead, but he cannot remember the message of the dreams. In superb lyrical passages a chorus of Greek captive women comments upon the struggle which is the cause of the tyrant's disquiet. The chorus beginning "In the great morning of the world" (1. 46) tells of the emergence of Freedom in Greece and traces its progress. This favorite theme of Shelley's is presented in an equally fine passage in "Ode to Liberty" but receives its fullest development in *A Philosophical View of Reform*. The chorus "Worlds on worlds are rolling ever" (1. 197) is a commentary upon the transience and incompleteness or falseness of human creeds.[50] The doom of Mohammedanism is

---

[49] Preface to *Hellas, Cambridge Works*, pp. 318-319.
[50] Shelley says in a note (*Oxford Works*, p. 478), "The popular notions of Christianity are represented in this chorus as true in their relation to the

predicted. Despite assurances from Hassan that the Turkish Empire, fortified by Moslem strength, is firm ("The lamp of our dominion still rides high" (1. 273)), Mahmud is gloomy: "Far other bark than ours were needed now / To stem the torrent of descending time" (11. 349-350). Hassan's subsequent account of the struggle between Turkish Moslems and the Greek forces reveals to Mahmud that his sympathies lie with the underdog Greeks. Four messengers bring news of Turkish reversals in land and sea battles. Ahasuerus, the Wandering Jew, symbol of undying rebellion in *Queen Mab*, appears now as a wise and prophetic philosopher. His counsel enables Mahmud to talk to the Phantom, who reveals that soon "Islam must fall" (1. 887). The last chorus, "The world's great age begins anew" (1. 1060), predicts that

> Another Athens shall arise,
>   And to remoter time
> Bequeath, like sunset to the skies,
>   The splendor of its prime;
> And leave, if nought so bright shall live,
> All earth can take or Heaven give
>   (11. 1084-1089).

The closing stanza suggests the possibility of the return of hate and death after the advent of a new Hellenic age. It is Shelley's view that liberty can never be secured so completely that it need not be guarded. The true significance of liberty is to be found only in the practices of liberty.

To sum up, Shelley's poems written after 1815 reflecting political thought are of a wide variety. They range from personal comments on Wordsworth and Napoleon to the subtle drama of *Prometheus Unbound*, from invectives against Sidmouth and Castlereagh to the choruses of *Hellas*. The 1819 group written in a popular style ("The Masque of Anarchy", "Lines Written

---

worship they superseded, and that which in all probability they will supersede, without considering their merits in a relation more universal. The first stanza contrasts immortality of the living and thinking beings which inhabit the planets, and to use a common and inadequate phrase, *clothe themselves in matter*, with the transience of the noblest manifestations of the external world."

during the Castlereagh Administration", etc.) forms a poetic parallel to pamphleteer literature. The lofty, visionary poems "Ode to Liberty", "Ode to Naples", and *Hellas* celebrate revolutions in progress. *The Revolt of Islam* pictures the ideals of liberty, fraternity, equality. *Prometheus Unbound* presents the spiritual rejuvenation of man. All of the ideas developed in the prose selections may be identified in the themes of the poems. Politically speaking, the poetry complements the prose works. Conversely, the prose works serve as commentaries upon the poetry.

V

SHELLEY'S POLITICAL INFLUENCE

It is clear that Shelley exercised little political influence during his lifetime. His ineffectiveness as a reformer was a source of profound disappointment to him. None of his political prose works was published under his own name. His more radical works either were suppressed or failed to find a publisher.[1] Reviews of his poetry in the journals of greatest influence were invariably hostile, though some, notably those in *Blackwood's Edinburgh Magazine*, were inclined to acknowledge his genius as a poet while deploring his views. His most extensive, though incomplete, commentary on politics, *A Philosophical View of Reform*, was not published until 1920. At all levels of endeavor his efforts for reform went unrewarded. Attempts at direct action in Ireland got nowhere. Attempts to influence public opinion through journalistic writings were fruitless. His unique talent for embodying the ideas of reform in poetry failed to earn him a reputation as a philosophical reformer.

[1] Shelley was apparently unwilling to become a martyr in the cause of freedom if martyrdom meant going to jail. When Daniel Hill, Shelley's Irish servant, was arrested in 1812 at Barnstaple, fined twenty pounds, and sentenced to jail for six months because he had attempted upon Shelley's instructions to circulate the anonymous *Declaration of Rights* and *The Devil's Walk*, Shelley provided Hill with prison comforts to the extent of fifteen shillings a week instead of revealing himself responsible for Hill's activities in an effort to secure his release. Additional evidence is Shelley's method of circulating *Queen Mab*. To avoid the danger of being imprisoned he presented copies of the poem "only to carefully chosen recipients, after first having removed all names and addresses which might lead to the identification of the author" (N. I. White, "Shelley and the Active Radicals of the Early Nineteenth Century", *South Atlantic Quarterly*, vol. XXIV (July, 1930), p. 250).

Despite the failure of his contemporaries to grant the literary recognition he merited, Shelley was not unknown. As an object of the hatred of the Tory press he received much adverse publicity. A minority of liberals, Leigh Hunt foremost among them, defended him. *Queen Mab*, shortly after its discovery in 1819 by Richard Carlile,[2] began a life of its own. White writes,

> the radical printer Richard Carlile . . . had asked and been refused permission to reprint it. He had respected Shelley's wishes, but his former employee William Clark was less scrupulous. He brought out and advertised [in 1821] two slightly variant editions, and the notorious radical piratical publisher William Benbow anonymously brought out still another edition under a false New York imprint.[3]

Shelley wanted to suppress these publications, which were selling "by the thousands",[4] because he felt that he should not be represented to the public by an early work, but owing to a court ruling that "books liable to conviction for blasphemy or sedition were not entitled to legal protection",[5] he could not do so. The government itself, however, took steps to suppress Clark's editions. Clark was indicted, bound himself to good behavior while awaiting trial, published a reply to *Queen Mab*, and at his trial on November 19, 1822, "made the most of this publication and of his willingness to surrender all copies of the offending book, but was nevertheless sentenced to four months' imprisonment".[6] The government was fighting a losing fight:

> *Queen Mab* became an important weapon in the arsenal of British working-class radicalism. . . . Within twenty years fourteen or more separate editions were issued by piratical radical publishers. The book took an honoured place with Volney's *Ruins of Empire*, Palmer's

---

[2] On November 3, 1819, Shelley wrote a letter in defense of Carlile, who had been fined heavily and sentenced to three years in prison for publishing Palmer's *Principles of Nature* and Paine's *Age of Reason*. See above, Chapter III, pp. 47-48.
[3] N. I. White, *Shelley*, vol. II, p. 304.
[4] Shelley's letter of June 16, 1821, to John Gisborne, *Julian Works*, vol. X, p. 278.
[5] N. I. White, *Shelley*, vol. II, p. 304.
[6] *Ibid.*, vol. II, p. 305.

Principles of Nature, Byron's *Cain*, and the works of Tom Paine in the little radical "libraries" constantly offered for sale.[7]

Whatever answer there may be to the question of Shelley's political influence is to be found in the posthumous growth of his literary reputation, a phenomenon as magical as the appearance of freedom amid tyranny in *The Masque of Anarchy*. White observes,

There were few signs of future admiration in the tone with which the British press received the news of Shelley's death [in 1822].

. . . .

Shelley's death had been greeted with the same factionalism – hatred from the Tories, championship from the radicals, and a fairly generous desire for fair play from the liberals – which had obscured his recognition during life.[8]

Since principally the radicals kept Shelley's name alive in the period immediately after his death, their identity and use of his works assume importance. They include such men as Carlile, Robert Owen, Henry Hetherington, and James Watson, who sought to bring about reform by challenging discriminatory actions of the government and by influencing the laboring class.

Carlile, after it became apparent that Clark's interest in publishing *Queen Mab* was commercial rather than political, "then published two editions of *Queen Mab* in 1822 and a third and fourth in 1823 and 1826, having meanwhile bought up and sold all that remained of Shelley's original edition".[9] He published an article praising Shelley in the December 15, 1826, issue of his *Republican* and another on the history of *The Revolt of Islam* in an 1829 issue of his *Lion*. Eight fellow radicals, sent to prison in 1825 for attempting to operate Carlile's printing shop while he was in prison, established and published *Newgate Magazine* (1825-1826), in which thirteen items on Shelley appeared. Still another edition of *Queen Mab* was brought out in 1832 by Carlile's wife and sons during his absence.[10]

Robert Owen (1771-1858), generally considered the founder of

[7] *Ibid.*, vol. II, p. 304.
[8] *Ibid.*, vol. II, pp. 389, 391.
[9] *Ibid.*, vol. II, p. 405.
[10] *Ibid.*, vol. II, pp. 405-406.

modern socialism, headed a group for whom *Queen Mab*, according to Medwin, became "almost a sort of Bible".[11] At the age of nineteen and as manager of a cotton mill employing five hundred persons he observed the impact of the industrial revolution upon wage earners and obtained a knowledge of the primary needs of his workers. In 1813 he persuaded his business partners to adopt socialistic as well as commercial principles in the operation of their mills at New Lanark, Scotland. The plan, which provided workers' benefits in the form of better housing, schools for children, and the privilege of purchasing goods at little more than cost, was successful both as a commercial venture and as a sociological experiment. The owners profited, and living conditions of the employees were improved. Interest in New Lanark spread throughout Britain and to Europe. Even Nicholas of Russia, afterwards Czar, took notice.

In 1815 Owen advanced demands for factory reforms which served to spearhead the movement. When hope faded that the government would institute such industrial reforms as he advocated, he set about organizing self-contained communities. In 1825 he founded New Harmony, Indiana. The design for this community was more radical than that of New Lanark. Features of the experiment were a contribution to the community from each member in the form of labor, communal ownership of property and distribution of goods, special schools in the arts and sciences, and a literary club for women. The project failed within three years owing to dissension over religion and the form of government, but Owen's doctrines had become popular with the working classes in England and were being widely published. Many organizations made him their spokesman. When he returned to England to continue fighting for reforms on a broad front, he found himself at the head of a group of societies that rapidly emerged as the trade union movement.[12] Owenite publications, 1821 to 1841, in which White has located Shelley items, mainly quotations, are *Cooperative Magazine and Monthly*

[11] See N. I. White, "Shelley and the Active Radicals of the Early Nineteenth Century", *South Atlantic Quarterly*, vol. XXIX (July, 1930), p. 260.
[12] For these and other facts concerning Owen, see the article on him in *Encyclopaedia Britannica* (1953), vol. XVI.

Herald (known as *London Cooperative Magazine* after 1830), *Magazine of Useful Knowledge and Cooperative Miscellany, Lancashire Cooperator, Crisis,* and *New Moral World*.[13]

Owen, like Shelley, was an outspoken critic of institutional religion and believed that religious toleration was essential to the welfare of society. Both Owen and Shelley viewed labor as the sole origin of wealth and therefore advocated reforms that would justly reward the laborer for his production and penalize those whose efforts were directed toward gaining possession of what others had produced. Shelley consistently advocated an economic system in which controls over the distribution of goods would prevent extremes of wealth and poverty. Other points on which Owen and Shelley agreed were abolition of child labor, education for the masses, and women's rights. Since Owen's political views parallel Shelley's extensively, it is hardly surprising that the Owenites took Shelley to heart and made him one of their own.

Hetherington, editor of *Poor Man's Guardian* (1831-1835) and with James Watson, of *Freethinkers' Information for the People* (1836), presented several brief Shelley quotations and extensively advertised *Queen Mab* in his periodicals; both men brought out additional pirated editions of the poem in 1839. In the same year Shelley was being quoted liberally in the *National, A Library for the People*, edited by W. J. Linton, where a biographical sketch and a sonnet of commendation also appeared.[14] Freedom of speech and press for the laboring classes was the primary objective of these men.

Hetherington and Watson are important largely because of the role they played in forcing the government to abandon its practice of using the Newspaper Stamp Tax and the law of blasphemous libel as weapons of discrimination against publications designed for the working man. Under these laws periodicals critical of the church or government were made prohibitively expensive for the workers, and publishers of radical religious and political opinion could be sued for libel and severely punished. Hetherington, Watson, and their colleagues employed the stratagem of forcing

[13] N. I. White, *Shelley*, vol. II, pp. 406-407.
[14] *Ibid.*, vol. II, p. 407.

the government to prosecute reputable as well as disreputable publishers. In a test case Edward Moxon, publisher of Shelley's collected works in 1839, was indicted for blasphemous libel for publishing a one-volume edition of the poems which included an unexpurgated *Queen Mab*, complete with "Notes". Though the government was reluctant to prosecute Moxon, "a gentleman and a respectable publisher",[15] he was tried on June 23, 1841, and found guilty but was not sentenced. The radicals, having won their point, did not press for judgment. The law was not used again to abridge the right of free expression in the press, though it remained on the statute books.[16] The trial was the type of action that Shelley had advocated in *A Philosophical View of Reform* as a means of calling into question dictatorial policies and of promoting peaceful reform.[17] It is ironical that the publication of this youthful work, which he tried to suppress in 1821, should become in 1841 the cause for the kind of maneuver he had urged in the fight for reform.

The story of Shelley's literary reputation between the time of his death in 1822 and the publication of his collected poems in 1839 is, by and large, the story of the popularity of *Queen Mab* with radical journalism. It was by far the best known of his works prior to his emergence as one of the major romantic poets. How to account for this phenomenon remains to some extent a matter of speculation. The poem contributed no ideas that could not have been derived from other sources. Tom Paine's works still spoke the people's idiom of revolution and reform; yet *Queen Mab* uniquely purveyed the spirit of the time. It would seem that the radicals found in the poem not an echo but an intensification

---

[15] *Ibid.*, vol. II, p. 408.
[16] The complete account of this episode appears in N. I. White, "Literature and the Law of Libel: Shelley and the Radicals of 1840-1842", *Studies in Philology*, vol. XXII (January, 1925), pp. 34-47. See also Sylva Norman, *Flight of the Skylark*, pp. 149-153.
[17] Shelley's statement in *A Philosophical View*: "The public opinion in England ought first to [be] excited to action, and the durability of those forms within which the oppressors intrench themselves brought perpetually to the test of its operation. No law or institution can last if this opinion be distinctly pronounced against it. For this purpose government ought to be defied, in cases of questionable result, to prosecute for political libel."

of their own enthusiasm for attack upon the twin objects of reform, church and state. It was a work that they gladly claimed. The net result of its popularity was to make Shelley appear to be more radical than he really was. The poem is the essence of youthful rebellion against outmoded religious and political doctrine and practice. If the later works which reflect his thought concerning the means as well as the ends of change in religion and government had been published with *Queen Mab*, he would have seemed to be a gradualist. A truer image would have prevailed.

Though the radicals' use of *Queen Mab* dominates the account of the early growth of Shelley's reputation, many other factors are discernible. Part of the journalistic attention to Shelley derived from a widespread, keen interest in Byron and centered upon anecdotes about Shelley as a member of Byron's circle.[18] Sir Timothy's efforts to blot out his son's name delayed Mary Shelley's publication of the poems, with biographical notes. The spirit of reform which resulted in the passage of the Reform Bill of 1832, began to modify the intellectual climate, so that a more objective consideration of Shelley became possible. Friends and relatives played various roles in the evolutionary growth of his fame. But the works themselves were the vital force. It was inevitable that they should begin to attract the readers for whom they were written.

At Oxford in 1829 Arthur Hallam, Richard Monckton Milnes, and Thomas Sutherland of the Cambridge Union Society debated the issue of Shelley's superiority as a poet to Byron with members of the Oxford Union Society. Although these Cambridge Apostles pressed their advantage – they had read Shelley and their opponents had not – the vote went in favor of Byron.[19] But Shelley's popularity was growing. Tennyson denied that Shelley's poetry had an immoral tendency, and Hallam, who was primarily

[18] A study of Shelley items in periodical literature leads White to conclude that "Nearly ten per cent of the total number of items were stimulated by an original interest in Byron and the *Liberal* [the short-lived periodical begun in 1822 by Shelley, Byron, and Leigh Hunt]" (N. I. White, *Shelley*, vol. II, p. 399).
[19] Sylva Norman, *Flight of the Skylark*, pp. 88-89.

responsible for having a copy of the original Pisan edition of *Adonais* reprinted at Cambridge in 1829,

included a long note [with his poem *Timbuctoo*] on ... [his] borrowing from "a magnificent passage in Mr. Shelley's *Alastor* ... that wonderful Poem, which cannot long remain in its present condition of neglect but would be marvelled at in time, for its great moral idea no less than for its poetic glory".[20]

In his essay on Bunyan (December, 1830) Macaulay, in spite of his failure to see that Shelley had produced "great work of the very highest rank in design and execution", acclaimed Shelley as Bunyan's equal in possessing an extraordinary talent for giving "to the abstract the interest of the concrete": "The spirit of Beauty, the Principle of Good, the Principle of Evil ... were ... intelligible forms, fair humanities, objects of love, of adoration, or of fear."[21] In 1832 the *Athenaeum* reviewed "in the highest terms that revolutionary *Mask of Anarchy* held back cautiously from the *Examiner* in 1819, and now published by Leigh Hunt. 'Genius', ... [wrote] the reviewer, 'must eventually have its triumph' ".[22]

The influence of Shelley upon Browning, who began reading him at the age of fourteen, is further evidence of the power of Shelley's poetry. William C. DeVane writes, "In 1826 when Browning discovered Shelley ... his poetic life properly began", and Browning never fully escaped from the effects of his early Shelley worship, reflected in *Pauline* (published anonymously in 1833) and in his temporary adoption of Shelley's vegetarianism, radicalism and atheism.[23]

Though artificial barriers to the publication of Shelley were slow to disappear – specifically, Sir Timothy's efforts to blot out his son's name and Mary's determination to guard his reputation, a mission taken over by his daughter-in-law, Lady Jane Shelley, upon Mary's death in 1851 – the Victorian bias which dominated

[20] *Ibid.*, pp. 87-88.
[21] Thomas B. Macaulay, *Miscellaneous Works of Lord Macaulay*, vol. I, pp. 826-828.
[22] Norman, *op. cit.*, p. 91.
[23] William C. DeVane, *The Shorter Poems of Robert Browning*, pp. xiv-xv.

the minds of many major literary figures was an important reason for the retardation of an understanding of Shelley and the spread of his influence. Mary herself became conservative in later life: "She regarded with horror the French revolution of 1848 and was thoroughly out of sympathy with the Chartists – some of whose leaders were doing their best to propagate the sale of *Queen Mab*." [24] Tennyson, who had been a Shelley enthusiast early in his career, set forth the dogma in his old age that "One must distinguish ... Keats, Shelley, and Byron from the great sage poets of all, [sic] who are both great thinkers and great artists, like Aeschylus, Shakespeare, Dante and Goethe".[25] Browning apparently paid for his change from Shelley idolatry to antipathy with a loss of unity of intellect. This does not imply that either idolatry or antipathy is preferable. It is simply further evidence, if any were needed, of the domination Shelley always held over those he touched. *Sordello* (1840) presents a study of Browning's divided mind in which at least one Browning scholar sees the influence of Browning's mother as the cause of his surrender of the spiritual freedom that he began to learn from Shelley.[26] Some Victorians, such as Carlyle and Charles Kingsley, were hostile toward Shelley, but the summit of Victorian critical thought concerning him was reached in Arnold's "beautiful and ineffectual angel".[27]

Obviously enough, Shelley's political thought – available mainly through his poetry, for *A Philosophical View of Reform* had not been published – was ineffectual among chief representatives of Victorianism. Browning was, perhaps, the only one of the group who might have adopted it. As a boy he did adopt Shelley's vegetarianism, atheism, and radicalism for a short time, but his later struggle to free himself from the influence of Shelley's poetic artistry, plus the strong influence of his mother's orthodoxy, separated him from any interest in political reform that he might have acquired.

Not all of the literati of Victorian England shared Arnold's

[24] N. I. White, *Shelley*, vol. II, p. 386.
[25] [Hallam Tennyson], *Alfred Lord Tennyson*, vol. II, p. 287.
[26] Betty Miller, *Robert Browning: A Portrait*, p. 140.
[27] N. I. White, *Shelley*, vol. II, p. 413.

appraisal, however. Swinburne and Shaw, who outlived the era, were strongly influenced by Shelley – Shaw by his political thought and Swinburne by both his politics and poetry. Unlike Browning, they welcomed the influence. Shaw had high praise for *Queen Mab* and *The Revolt of Islam*. Swinburne was delighted to find parallels to Shelley in his own life and works. Ruskin, a mid-Victorian, often made derogatory remarks about Shelley similar to those of Tennyson but, like Tennyson, was a Shelley enthusiast in his youth. His views on Shelley fluctuated throughout his life, and his writings on political economy provide an interesting comparison with Shelley's ideas on the subject. Finally, the Shelley Society (1886-1895), though a source of much of what has been called the "Shelley legend", played its part in the study and spread of Shelley's political ideas.

Shelley's influence upon Ruskin took many curious turns. At the beginning of his career Ruskin read and imitated Shelley's poetry. He wrote *Farewell* (1841), a long poem to Adèle Domecq, "in the style of Shelley", and it became "a particular 'pet' of its author".[28] Looking back in later years Ruskin disparaged his early Shelley enthusiasm:

In ... 1836, I took to reading Shelley ... and wasted much time over *The Sensitive Plant* and *Epipsychidion*; and I took a good deal of harm from *him*, in trying to write lines like "prickly and pulpous and blistered and blue"; or "it was a little lawny islet by anemone and vi'let, – like mosaic paven", etc.[29]

This statement, a part of Ruskin's account of his early "days of ferment", would indicate either that he never perceived any of the real values of Shelley or that he did not intend it to be taken literally and seriously. Other statements in a similar vein, which he made from time to time, suggest, however, that it may represent a considered opinion. In view of his ultimate achievement as a poet it can be understood why he felt that his study of Shelley's poetry had been a bad influence, but it is difficult to

---

[28] *The Works of John Ruskin*, vol. II, p. xxii.
[29] *Ibid.*, vol. XXXV, p. 183. The quotation is taken from *Praeterita*, vol. I, published in 1886.

see why he felt that some other course would have been more helpful.

There is, surprisingly, a substantial body of comment scattered through Ruskin's works which is in conflict with his disapproving statements about Shelley. The reason for the contradiction probably is to be found in his unstable mental condition, an aspect of his life which biographers touch upon lightly. One commentator believes that "much of the contradictory element in Ruskin's writing arises from his sheer love of shock" – that is, a desire to make rash, dramatic statements which will startle his readers.[30] Be that as it may, Ruskin shows, in spite of much evidence to the contrary, an understanding of Shelley which is considerably superior to that of contemporaries such as Arnold and Tennyson.

In an article on the proposed Scott monument in Edinburgh, which appeared in *The Architectural Magazine* in 1838, Ruskin commends Shelley for his ability "to excite admiration of any given character ... by pointing to the great first cause ... which excited and fostered within it that feeling which is the essence and glory of all noble minds".[31] He observes that such a feeling is "indefinable except in the words of one who felt it above many: –

> 'The desire of the moth for the star,
> Of the night for the morrow,
> The devotion to something afar
> From the sphere of our sorrow' ".[32]

Most importantly, Ruskin reflects a spiritual kinship to Shelley by identifying himself with political reform, a primary motive of Shelley's genius. In the essay *Fiction, Fair and Foul* (1880) he says, speaking of himself, Rousseau, Shelley, Byron, and Turner:

> in the whole group of us, glows volcanic instinct of Astraean justice returning not to, but up out of, the earth, which will not at all suffer us to rest any more in Pope's serene "whatever is, is right"; but holds, on the contrary, profound conviction that about ninety-nine hundredths of whatever at present is, is wrong: conviction making four of us, according to our several manners, leaders of revolution for the poor,

[30] John T. Fain, *Ruskin and the Economists*, p. 82.
[31] *The Works of John Ruskin*, vol. I, pp. 251-252.
[32] *Ibid.*, vol. I, p. 252. Ruskin's quotation is taken from Shelley's lines "To – ", written in 1821.

and declarers of political doctrine monstrous to the ears of mercenary mankind; and driving the fifth [Turner], less sanguine, into mere painted-melody of lament over the fallacy of Hope and the implacableness of Fate.[33]

This passage, reflecting Ruskin's knowledge and appreciation of Shelley's political thought and activity, raises two questions, which may or may not be related: (1) what were the sources of Ruskin's acquaintance with Shelley's political doctrine, and (2) what influence, if any, did Shelley have upon his politics?

It would seem that no completely satisfactory answers to these questions can be devised. A search through the index of Ruskin's *Works* (edited by E. T. Cook and Alexander Wedderburn) produces few references to his reading of, or about, Shelley, and Ruskin scholarship is, apparently, no more helpful. Ruskin refers to various poems of Shelley, but much of what he says about them is derogatory, as may be seen above. His further comment in *Praeterita* (1886) concerns his reading of *The Revolt of Islam* and *Prometheus Unbound* in 1836:

The perseverance with which I tried to wade through the *Revolt of Islam*, and find out (I never did, and don't know to this day) who revolted against whom, or what, was creditable to me; and the *Prometheus* really made me understand something of Aeschylus.[34]

If this statement may be taken at face value, we have Ruskin's word that he learned nothing of Shelley's political thought from either *The Revolt* or *Prometheus*, though these two long poems embody just about all of it in one way or another. No reader who finds *The Revolt* tiresome and opaque deserves censure, but *Prometheus* is another matter. Ruskin may have profited from reading these works again in the fifty-year interval between 1836 and 1886, but if so, he has neglected to inform the readers of his autobiography of the fact. In view of the quantity of reading, writing, and lecturing that he did throughout his life and of his perception of Shelley's passion for reform, it is almost impossible to believe that he did not study Shelley extensively.

Lacking evidence that would tell which works informed Ruskin

[33] *Ibid.*, vol. XXXIV, p. 343.
[34] *Ibid.*, vol. XXXV, p. 183.

of Shelley's "volcanic instinct of . . . justice" and "[declaration] of political doctrine monstrous to the ears of mercenary mankind", we are left with the general conclusion that he had read sufficiently in, and about Shelley to understand and esteem his deepest source of strength, i.e., a passion for political reform. It would be impossible to say that Ruskin had read all of Shelley's works that were available at the time, but his true appraisal of Shelley suggests that he had read widely, to include the important poems, prose tracts, and biographical material. The only important work that would not have been available to him was *A Philosophical View of Reform*. Dowden's condensed version did not appear until 1888 in *Transcripts and Studies*, and the work itself was not published until 1920.

Since the answer to the question concerning sources of Ruskin's acquaintance with Shelley as a political reformer can be made only in general terms, it follows that the answer to the question of Shelley influences, if any, upon Ruskin's politico-economic doctrine must be equally generalized. In the absence of Ruskin's acknowledgments of indebtedness or of internal evidence which would point to his borrowing from specific Shelley works, we can do no more than observe parallels or similarities where they exist. The fact that Ruskin's works on political economy are frequently embellished with moralizing observations of a religious cast and are, in a sense, reactions against the standard doctrine of the day as propounded by Mill and other specialists in economics would seem to promise that any comparison with Shelley's ideas would be an exercise in futility. But the fundamental question to be considered is whether or not Ruskin's politico-economic thought would have been exactly as it is if Shelley had never lived. The answer is probably no. A resume of Ruskin's ideas on the subject will help to show why.

Ruskin's works on political economy are *Unto this Last* (1862), *Time and Tide* (1867), *Munera Pulveris* (1872), and *Fors Clavigera* (1878).[35] They are fragmentary in that they do not provide a complete, systematic discussion of political economy

---

[35] The contents of these works first appeared as essays and letters which were published in magazines and newspapers before they were collected.

but offer instead criticism of existing thinking and practices, and suggest changes. They are also overlapping and to some extent repetitious. *Unto this Last* contains the core of Ruskin's ideas, which he derived from a study of the classics. *Munera Pulveris* is, in a general way, Ruskin's attempt to outline a plan of social economy, and *Time and Tide* is designed, also loosely, to suggest how his principles would be applied in society. *Fors Clavigera* is "a puzzling miscellany" made up of letters which Ruskin wrote "for all 'fellow-workmen' with him, all labourers in the vineyard; including . . . 'masters, pastors, and princes' no less than the rank and file".[36] It should be noted that Ruskin had abandoned the narrow, orthodox, institutional Christianity of his early years by the time he began writing on political economy. His works which were based upon, or which developed, moral principles had become expressions of his religion of humanity. Since political economy as he saw it must be governed by moral principles, his works in this field are often missionary in spirit.

Unto this Last (1862) is made up of "Four Essays on the First Principles of Political Economy" which originally appeared in *Cornhill Magazine* in 1860. Though it is usually considered as an attack on existing doctrine, it contains the bases of all of Ruskin's politico-economic ideas and hence will suffice for purposes of comparison, because it is representative.

The first chapter, which consists of the essay "The Roots of Honour", presents Ruskin's view that the economic world must abandon the dog-eat-dog principle of competition upon which it currently functioned – a principle not only defined and studied, but advocated, by economists because it seemed to them the inevitable, and therefore right, law of commerce. In practice this principle means that an employer must strive to get the most productive work out of an employee for the least wages possible. An employee who is not satisfied with his wages is free to find work elsewhere. An employer has no obligation to retain an employee when there is no demand for what the employee produces. The employer may, of course, dismiss him for other reasons, but economic necessity forces dismissal when demand

[36] E. T. Cook, *The Life of John Ruskin*, vol. II, pp. 313-314.

decreases or disappears. Economists defended this system by saying that it stimulated maximum production, a condition beneficial to society and consequently to the worker himself. Ruskin's answer is that this would be true only if an employee were "an engine of which the motive power was steam".[37] He contends that the best work is done by employees whose wages are regular and are not dependent upon an uncertain demand for their services. In such situations the motivation for the workers' productivity is not only wages but pride in their occupation as well. An employee whose work is not continuous needs higher wages than one whose work has no interruptions.

Ruskin's final objection to accepted commercial practice is that "the merchant is presumed to act always selfishly".[38] His proposed change is "to discover a kind of commerce which is not exclusively selfish".[39] He is in effect proposing that commerce be governed by ethical principles similar to those which bind the professions. Commercial institutions, he believes, should be conducted upon principles of honor similar to those which prevail in the operation of a ship:

as the captain of a ship is bound to be the last man to leave his ship in case of wreck, and to share his last crust with the sailors in case of famine, so the manufacturer, in any commercial crisis or distress is bound to take the suffering of it with his men, and even to take more of it for himself than he allows his men to feel.[40]

The second chapter, the essay "The Veins of Wealth", begins with an attack upon the "science of getting rich":

the art of becoming "rich", in the common sense, is not absolutely nor finally the art of accumulating much money for ourselves, but also of contriving that our neighbors shall have less. In accurate terms, it is "the art of establishing the maximum inequality in our own favour".[41]

Ruskin points out that it cannot be shown in the abstract that

[37] *The Works of John Ruskin*, vol. XVII, p. 29.
[38] *Ibid.*, vol. XVII, p. 38.
[39] *Ibid.*, vol. XVII, pp. 38-39.
[40] *Ibid.*, vol. XVII, p. 42.
[41] *Ibid.*, vol. XVII, p. 46.

such inequality is either advantageous or harmful to the nation and that since this is true, "The ... assumption that such inequalities are necessarily advantageous, lies at the root of most of the popular fallacies on the subject of political economy".[42] He concludes that the method by which inequalities of wealth come about and the purposes to which they are applied determine whether or not they are beneficial to society. Inequalities justly established are a benefit. Those produced by the middleman in commerce are evil if the middleman unjustly holds back wealth produced by others for his own benefit in the process of transferring it from a producer to a consumer. Ruskin acknowledges that the middleman has a valid function in the economy by efficiently serving the needs of both producers and consumers.

Having discussed distribution of wealth, Ruskin concludes the chapter by pointing out that since wealth is not money but is in essence power over men, "persons themselves *are* the wealth":

it may be discovered that the true veins of wealth are purple – and not in Rock but in Flesh – perhaps even that the final outcome and consummation of all wealth is in the producing as many as possible full-breathed, bright-eyed, and happy-hearted human creatures.[43]

The third chapter of *Unto this Last*, "Qui Judicatis Terram", discusses the problem of economic justice in society. Ruskin argues that the only just payment for labor is labor. A completely just system would require that persons receiving the benefit from an hour of work by a laborer must repay him with an equal amount of their own work according to the benefit each received. Since this is impractical, the laborer is paid in coin which gives him command over national work. But the coin which the laborer receives for the hour he must spend doing a specific job will get him only a half hour of work, or much less, from someone else: "Any given craftsman will always be willing to give an hour of his own work in order to receive command over half an hour, or even much less, of national work."[44] Ruskin then points out that exact equality is impossible because some men are superior

[42] *Ibid.*, vol. XVII, pp. 46-47.
[43] *Ibid.*, vol. XVII, pp. 55-56.
[44] *Ibid.*, vol. XVII, pp. 66-67.

to others, but he insists upon his main contention that national economic advantage depends upon the payment of just, or fair, wages.

In the last chapter, "Ad Valorem", Ruskin discusses production, value, exchange, and profit. He believes that "the manner and issue of consumption ... are the real tests of production. Production does not consist in things labouriously made, but in things serviceably consumable".[45] Thus the products of labor are beneficial only if they lead to an enrichment of life and an expansion of the capacity for living. The extent to which something is "serviceably consumable" determines its value. Only those things are valuable which cultivate life. The general law of exchange which should govern commerce is that "There must be advantage on both sides"; this rules out profit because "Whatever material gain follows exchange, for every *plus* there is a precisely equal *minus*." [46]

The concept advanced in "The Veins of Wealth" that good people constitute the wealth of a nation is re-emphasized:

There is no wealth but life. ... That country is the richest which nourishes the greatest number of noble and happy human beings; that man is richest who, having perfected the functions of his own life to the utmost, has also the widest helpful influence, both personal, and by means of his possessions, over the lives of others.[47]

One does not have to be an economist to see that many of Ruskin's ideas – particularly those dealing with the mechanics of commerce and industry – would not stand up under close analysis. But his basic principles are as clear as they are radical, and they are strikingly similar to some of Shelley's. Both Shelley and Ruskin would have the economy governed by principles of honor, or fair play, which assume natural, or equal, rights of individuals. Individuals, in turn, would have to discipline their own lives with the same ethical principles. They are in agreement that extremes of wealth and poverty in a nation – the few extremely wealthy as opposed to the many extremely poor – are manifesta-

---

[45] *Ibid.*, vol. XVII, p. 104.
[46] *Ibid.*, vol. XVII, pp. 91, 93.
[47] *Ibid.*, vol. XVII, p. 104.

tions of misdirected theory and practice in political economy. They believe that national interest is best served by those measures which would bring the greatest good to the greatest number. Both attack the defenses made for great fortunes. Ruskin points out that unrestricted competition, which results in a few great accumulations of wealth at the expense of the poor, is not an inevitable and unchangeable social principle and that the assumption that it is leads to disaster. The richest country is the one having "the greatest number of noble and happy human beings" rather than the one having the greatest stores of goods. Shelley observes that the great fortunes had their beginnings in usurpation and conquest and that the unrestricted economic power inherent in them causes them to snowball, further increasing the heavy burdens of the poor in the process. Both Shelley and Ruskin value the welfare of the masses above cultivation of fine arts if such cultivation depends upon the patronage of the wealthy. In *An Address to the Irish People* (1812) Shelley says,

are not the arts very inferior things to virtue and happiness? – the man would be very dead to all generous feelings who would rather see pretty pictures and statues than a million free and happy men.[48]

Though equitable distribution of wealth is a basic doctrine in the economic thinking of Shelley and Ruskin, it is not to be identified with equal distribution. They agree that economic inequalities are inevitable and just, provided that they are the result of productive labor. Inequalities built upon possession rather than production of goods are what must be prevented. Thus they have similar doctrines of work and value. Workers produce wealth, and consequently the economy of a nation must be designed to reward and encourage the producers and penalize the nonproducers. Utility becomes the measure of value.

A final parallel between Shelley and Ruskin is the participation of each in a utopian settlement project, though the term "utopian" is much more applicable to Ruskin's St. George's Guild than to the Tremadoc establishment in Wales with which Shelley was

[48] *Shelley's Prose*, p. 52.

briefly associated. In regard to Ruskin's project his biographer, E. T. Cook, observes,

> Ruskin's schemes, like those of other builders of Utopia, were large and picturesque. St. George's Company, or Guild, was to embrace all holy and humble men of heart. Its main effort was designed to show "how much food-producing land might be recovered by well-applied labour from the barren or neglected districts of nominally cultivated countries". It was to purchase land and to employ labourers upon it "under the carefullest supervision and with every proper means of mental instruction".[49]

A detailed account of Ruskin's plans for the Guild [50] would serve no useful purpose. A few of its main features will suffice. Ruskin contributed seven thousand pounds to establish the Guild in 1871, but its license to operate was not granted until 1878. The chief administrative officer was to be a "Master" whose authority would be absolute. Intermediate officers were to be "Marshals" (district managers) and "Landlords" (wealthy men who would contribute to the support of the Guild). "Young people bred on old estates" were to make up the laboring force, and their leaders were to be "veteran soldiers". Fixed rents would be reinvested in land improvements. Adequate and appropriate housing, schools, and libraries were to be provided for all members. Social class distinctions were to be maintained. Though the organization was to be primarily an agricultural economy, life was to be refined, and all useful crafts were to be studied.

The Tremadoc enterprise [51] had its beginning in 1807 when Parliament granted W. A. Madocks the sandy marshes that were to be reclaimed from the sea. By 1812, the year Shelley arrived, the project was almost complete. Two thousand acres had been reclaimed, and the model village of Tremadoc had been built on them. The only thing remaining to be done was the completion of a large dike which would shut out the sea entirely. But before Shelley arrived storms had damaged much of the work already

---

[49] Cook, *op. cit.*, vol. II, p. 333.
[50] Cook provides such an account, *op. cit.*, vol. II, pp. 333 ff. The summary which follows is based upon this reference.
[51] N. I. White, *Shelley*, vol. I, pp. 254 ff. is the source of information given on the subject.

done, and Madocks lacked the resources to make repairs and complete the job. He was seeking aid in the surrounding territory, and Shelley, who had just returned from his Irish venture, joined in helping solicit funds. It was a kind of philanthropic enterprise which was ideally suited to his youthful enthusiasm.

On the surface, differences between Shelley and Ruskin seem to be more impressive than similarities. Ruskin founded St. George's Guild when he was fifty-two, and his writings on reform of the political economy came toward the end of his life. Shelley was twenty when he joined the Tremadoc enterprise, and the evidence seems to indicate that he would not have done so had the opportunity come several years later when he was writing his major poetry. Much of Ruskin's work has a religious, and even evangelical, tone, though he had abandoned orthodox Christianity. (His unorthodox religion was the reason given by Rosie La Touche for refusing to marry him – but, guided by her mother, she was looking for reasons to say no.) Shelley's political works, on the other hand, even his most fervent ones, lack piety and often reveal a hostility toward institutional religion. There is no indication that Ruskin wished to reform the government beyond changing its political economy. Shelley was a republican. He believed that radically changing the political structure was the principal means of improving the economy. And Ruskin's respect and reverence for "veteran soldiers" would have appalled Shelley.

Yet Ruskin was right in recognizing that he was an ideological kinsman of Rousseau, Shelley, and Byron. He could not be indifferent to the degradation and misery of poverty which he saw around him. He saw the importance and necessity of changing economic practices. He expressed his views and supported them with his own finances in the face of opposition and ridicule, some of which no doubt was not undeserved.

Ruskin's indebtedness to Shelley cannot be clearly defined. He prepared to write upon the subject of political economy not by reading Shelley but by studying Plato's *Republic*, and Xenophon's *Economist*, and the works of other classical writers, both Greek and Roman. His study of contemporary economists was for the purpose of making his attack. There is a missionary spirit pervading his work, however, which carries the authority of conviction. It is much the same as that found in Shelley's political works. This is not to say that Ruskin's fervor would not have existed without Shelley, but it seems almost certain that it was reinforced by his reading of Shelley. Shelley's influence, then, upon Ruskin is what may be called the influence of reinforcement. It is highly probable – almost a certainty – that Ruskin's study of Shelley strengthened his resolution to proceed with the fight for his unpopular program of politico-economic reform.

Shelley's influence upon Swinburne does not need to be established. Swinburne's republican poetry, most of which is to be found in his best work, *Songs before Sunrise* (1871), reflects intense sympathy for world-wide revolution. He was preoccupied with the Italian revolutionary movement, whose leader, Giuseppe Mazzini, he had met, and addressed much of his poetry to the subject. But when the French republic was proclaimed in 1870, in the manner of Shelley "He instantly hailed the formation of the government ... as the arrival of a French millennium, and within two days he had composed and sent to press his long *Ode on the Proclamation of the French Republic*".[52] Napoleon III became for him a special object of denunciation.

It is generally recognized that Swinburne's passion for political reform was that of the idealist and spectator. He never attempted to participate as actively in a revolutionary movement as Shelley did; consequently, his political poems have an intellectual or philosophical quality and are only indirectly related to current events. Yet his feeling was intense and genuine. One of his biographers, Edmund Gosse, extracts from five poems in *Songs before Sunrise* what he believes to be the essence of Swinburne's political philosophy: "They [the poems] establish that the summit of freedom is that condition in which the Spirit of Humanity acts and moves with the severest ethical propriety." [53] This concept of freedom is in accord with Shelley's views.

As a controversialist (in this instance minus the Rabelaisian

---

[52] Edmund Gosse, *The Life of Algernon Charles Swinburne*, p. 186.
[53] *Ibid.*, p. 194. The five poems are "Mater Triumphalis", "Prelude", "Epilogue", "The Litany of Nations", and "Hertha".

invective) Swinburne wrote an impassioned, Shelley-like essay, *Of Loyalty and Liberty* (1866),[54] attacking the view of Carlyle and Ruskin that obedience and loyalty without freedom of choice are highest virtues. The task was one that Swinburne appears to have relished. He observes that loyalty is a virtue only when there is liberty to choose or withhold loyalty and that "It is doubtless quite possible that a freeman should not be loyal; but it is quite impossible that a slave should be".[55] After exposing the skeleton of their contention by careful analysis, he disposes of it:

According to this doctrine there must be no right, we are told, of refusal or compliance according to our own will or conscience; our part is obedience, and entire obedience, and nothing but obedience. And yet they tell us that loyalty is a virtue! What virtue can there be in giving what we have no choice but to give? in yielding that which we have neither might nor right to withhold?[56]

Swinburne's accord with Shelley is reflected in a letter to his sister, telling of his plan to write "a short memoir of Shelley and reviews of his works for Chambers's *Encyclopaedia*":

I must say it is too funny – not to say uncanny – how much there is in common between us two: born in exactly the same [class], sent to Eton at exactly the same age, cast out of Oxford ... and holding and preaching the same general views in the poems which made us famous.[57]

Swinburne's view of what he had in common with Shelley shows the nature of Shelley's influence upon him. Though admittedly biased in Shelley's favor, he produced some of the most accurate observations concerning Shelley's works to be found in nineteenth-century criticism. His main weakness as a critic, it has been said, is his inability to discuss one author fairly and justly without at the same time being unfair and unjust to another, and this is true of his treatment of Shelley when he compares him with Byron.

---

[54] This tract was written in 1866 but was "privately printed in 1909, with notes by Mr. Edmund Gosse". See Edward Thomas, *Algernon Charles Swinburne*, p. 115.
[55] *The Complete Works of Algernon Charles Swinburne*, vol. XVI, p. 43.
[56] *Ibid.*, vol. XVI, p. 47.
[57] Mrs. Disney Leith, *Algernon Charles Swinburne*, p. 221.

His statements concerning Shelley's political writings in his article *Percy Bysshe Shelley* are revealing:

> The value of Shelley's prose writings is almost purely subjective; they would have no interest whatever for any imaginable reader if they threw no light on the character which helped to shape and to colour, to modify and to quicken, the genius of a poet. As a thinker he was just and generous rather than original and profound ... and his style is generally rather than particularly good.[58]

These observations are, on the whole, fair and discerning, though they do not expose any real secrets. Shelley did not claim to have originated the principles of government and economics which he presents in the pamphlets. He gives credit to his sources. The pamphlets represent his attempt to participate in the revolutionary movement at a time when it was dangerous to do so – something that Swinburne never did, even in less dangerous times. Swinburne is right in saying that the prose writings would never have attracted notice except as commentaries upon the development of Shelley's poetic genius. He is also right in his judgment that Shelley's style is generally, but not particularly, good, though it would appear to be at least good enough to rank with his own. He observes the generous, humane quality of Shelley which the tracts disclose. His appraisal of Shelley's prose writings is sound, by and large, but sound only from the viewpoint of literary criticism. And this calls attention to Swinburne's deficiency.

As a political revolutionary Swinburne is sometimes called a pseudo-Shelley, and in a sense he is. His works on reform possess the fervor of Shelley's but lack the vitality. He did not have the talent to equal Shelley as a poet under any circumstances, but the significant difference between himself and Shelley in the field of political reform is the absence from his works of the kind of prose writings he found in Shelley's. From his viewpoint (that of literary criticism) Shelley's tracts truly have no interest except as they contribute to an understanding of his poetic development. But it is certain that without them and what they stand for, his poems would not be what they are. The impotence of Swinburne's

[58] *The Complete Works of Algernon Charles Swinburne*, vol. XV, pp. 338-339.

political idealism is rooted in his nonparticipation in the political affairs of the day. His physical handicap (epilepsy) probably made active participaton of the sort Shelley engaged in an impossibility for him, but there is no evidence that he ever tried to work actively under any conditions for the cause he championed poetically.

The Shelley Society (1886-1895) is of incidental significance to a consideration of Shelley's political influence. The scholarly majority of its members were politically orthodox, but it contained a few socialists, among them Geoge Bernard Shaw, advocate of Fabian socialism, and Edward B. Aveling and Eleanor Marx Aveling, advocates of Marxian socialism.[59] The Avelings deserve notice because of their essay *Shelley and Socialism,* part of which was read as a lecture at a meeting of the Shelley Society on December 14, 1887.[60] And the fiery, colorful, highly original Shaw is the most scintillating of all the Shelley-influenced writers.

Before examining the Avelings' study of Shelley, one should say a word concerning socialism in England in the late nineteenth century. The resurgence of the socialist movement after a period of quiescence dates from the appearance of Karl Marx's *Das Kapital* in 1867. Previously, the trade unionists and their allies had become identified with Chartism, a movement which embodied the objectives of the working class and sought reform of the election laws. The Chartists had made liberal use of Shelley's doctrine in formulating their aims, but unlike Shelley they were militant. In 1848 the government, fearing a rebellion by the workers, placed the Duke of Wellington in command of a special force to suppress revolution. The few riots that did occur were easily quelled, and the Chartist movement came to an end.

Toward the close of the century the radicals began to see in

[59] Marxian and Fabian socialism, their background, and their relation to each other and to Shelley and Shaw are discussed at length in the useful study *Shelley and Bernard Shaw: A Study in Late Nineteenth Century Socialism* (1948), an unpublished thesis by Elmore E. Stokes, Jr., presented to the faculty of the graduate school of The University of Texas in partial fulfillment of the requirements for the degree of Master of Arts. This work is in the library of The University of Texas.
[60] The entire essay appeared in the April, 1888, issue of *To-Day* magazine. Part I, the part presented as a lecture, was published in *The Shelley Society's Papers,* vol. I, part II, pp. 180-203.

Marx's doctrines, expounded in the *Communist Manifesto* in 1847 (by Marx and Friedrich Engels) and in *Das Kapital* the theoretical foundation which would serve their purposes. Marx's interpretation of history as a struggle between the ruling and working classes could be projected into the future. The extremes of wealth and poverty caused by the capitalist system, in which the ruling class (owners and managers) take wealth from the workers in the form of profits, would grow larger and larger. As a result the system would inevitably come to a violent end. At that point the proletariat would be ready to assume control, and its rule would begin. The two classes would be dissolved into one productive class, and everyone would then obtain his equitable share of the economy.

The Fabian Society, founded in 1884, had the same materialistic objective as Marxist socialism: an equitable share of the nation's wealth for each worker. But it rejected the Marxian doctrine of violence as a means of obtaining this end and held that the goal would be reached gradually through evolutionary change of social institutions. It attracted a large number of influencial socialists, such as H. G. Wells, Bertrand Russell, and Henry S. Salt. One of its most important members was, of course, Shaw. Some of its later members, Ramsay MacDonald, Hugh Dalton, Harold J. Laski, and Sir Stafford Cripps, became leaders of the British Labour Party.[61]

Marxian and Fabian socialism were both flourishing during the middle 1880's when the Shelley Society was formed. Though most of the Marxists derived little or nothing from Shelley's political doctrine, they admired his revolutionary spirit. The Avelings, however, were Shelley enthusiasts, and their essay *Shelley and Socialism* was designed to show that Shelley's views fully supported their cause:

we have thought that there may be some interest in a study of Shelley and his writings by those who hold economic and political ideas that are in the main identical with his.[62]

[61] For an account of Marxian and Fabian socialism in England, see Stokes, *op. cit.*, pp. 180 ff.
[62] Edward Aveling and Eleanor Marx Aveling, "Shelley and Socialism", *The Shelley Society's Papers*, vol. I, part II, p. 181.

After this introduction, it is a foregone conclusion that the Avelings will find evidence to prove that Shelley was a socialist – not only a socialist but a teacher of socialism. They proceed to summarize their concept of the meaning of socialism. It is in essence the Marxian doctrine of the class struggle. The conclusion of their summary is of special interest because it concerns the revolution which the Marxists claimed would inevitably occur:

lastly ... the approaching change in "civilized" society will be a revolution, or in the words of Shelley "the system of human society as it exists at present must be overthrown from the foundations".[63]

The quotation from Shelley which the Avelings claim puts him in accord with Marxist doctrine is taken from a letter addressed to Leigh Hunt, dated May 1, 1820. It is noteworthy that they do not explain the means by which the socialists believed the revolution would be accomplished, nor do they interpret Shelley's statement. When Shelley spoke of overthrowing the current social system, he was not advocating violence as were the Marxists. The remainder of their lengthy essay is an attempt to show by references to Shelley's life and works that he formulated and taught the principles basic to the Marxian socialist movement.

The Avelings are successful in showing that Shelley's humanitarian objectives are similar to those of theoretical socialism, but they gloss over the important problem of the means by which the objectives are to be attained. Shelley's lifelong advocacy of a slow, evolutionary, nonviolent change of political institutions is contrary to the dogmas of Marxian socialism. It is in this large area that the Avelings distort Shelley's political doctrines. Their techniques of distortion are vague ambiguities and omissions. What they say is generally true, but the truth which they neglect to disclose would falsify much of the impression they seek to leave.

The Fabian socialists, on the other hand, were fundamentally in harmony with Shelley's political ideals, and when the Fabian Society was in its prime, Fabianism and Shavianism were largely the same thing. In other words, Shelley was Shaw's kind of socialist, and Shaw vigorously said as much:

[63] *Ibid.*, vol. I, part II, pp. 181-182.

When Bernard Shaw rose in one of the scholarly meetings of the Shelley Society and declared that he had joined "because, like Shelley, I was a Socialist, an atheist, and a vegetarian", by his own account he "scandalized many of the members", . . . but at the same time he gave an index to the Shelleyan spirit and enthusiasm which pervaded a large segment of English socialism at the time.[64]

Shaw was attracted to Shelley more by Shelley's revolt against all conventional social forms than by specific political ideas, though much, if not all, of Shaw's doctrine parallels Shelley's. Shaw's spirited attacks upon conventionality were similar to Shelley's in fervor and clarity. Both Shelley and Shaw took keen delight in forcefully advocating views which they knew were shocking to their contemporaries, but Shaw, unlike Shelley, always injected comedy designed to call attention to himself that had the effect of making him a great original. This is not to say that he lacked Shelley's sincerity and conviction in holding unorthodox views, but the wit and comedy of his expression disarmed his adversaries. Although Shaw made bitter enemies, there was no serious feeling that he was a dangerous radical who ought to be suppressed at all costs. In fact, the idea that he could be suppressed probably seemed ludicrous to those who might have wished to try. As Archibald Henderson, Shaw's biographer, observes, "Shelley profoundly influenced Shaw's thought and conduct, but probably exerted upon him no literary influence whatever." [65] Shaw's comments upon *Queen Mab* and *The Revolt of Islam* serve to illustrate this point. At the first regular meeting of the Shelley Society on April 14, 1886, Shaw observed that

"*Queen Mab* was a perfectly original poem on a great subject. Throughout the whole poem Shelley showed a remarkable grasp of facts, anticipating also the modern view that sociological problems are being worked out independently of the conscious interference of man."[66]

---

[64] Stokes, *op. cit.*, p. 1, quoting George Bernard Shaw, *Prefaces*, preface to Immaturity, p. 632.
[65] Archibald Henderson, *George Bernard Shaw: Man of the Century*, p. 778.
[66] *Ibid.*, pp. 147-148.

His reply to violent, intolerant criticism of *The Revolt of Islam* by A. G. Ross at a meeting on April 13, 1887, was that

a poem ought to be didactic, and ought to be in the nature of a political treatise – for poetry was the most artistic way of teaching those things which a poet ought to teach.[67]

The significance of such Shavian opinions is, as Sylva Norman observes, that Shaw

is himself the perfect Fabian who cares more for Socialism than for art. His choice is Shelley the conspirator, not Shelley the poet. The latter he would readily tear for his bad verses, which get in the way of maxims.[68]

The most famous trait of Shaw's conduct, his vegetarianism, was derived from Shelley. Though it is really unrelated to Shelley's politics, Shaw made it a part of his own political creed. The Fabians, reacting to the impact of Darwin, adapted the principle of evolution to their conception of the way in which social institutions must be changed. Shelley's idea was similar though he was pre-Darwinian. Shaw, following Samuel Butler's lead, rejected Darwin's theory that chance happenings account for the various forms of life, on the grounds that it removed mind and morals from the universe. He substituted a "Religion of Creative Evolution" based upon a mystical attitude toward a Universal Spirit and Life Force, which were conceived of as irresistibly driving the human race and the world toward a loftier and more refined state of being.[69] Shaw resembled Shelley in being concerned primarily with the spiritual or intellectual nature of man. The political doctrines of the Fabians were designed to accommodate and aid this evolutionary process of social amelioration, which was impelled by the Universal Spirit. Shaw, whose sense of morality was strict and puritanical as well as humanitarian, fitted vegetarianism into this Fabian outlook: "man should recognize and respect the rights and integrity of other fellow-creatures, human and animal".[70] For this reason, meat-eating to Shaw was a

[67] *Ibid.*, p. 151.
[68] Norman, *op. cit.*, p. 272.
[69] See George Bernard Shaw, *Back to Methuselah*, revised edition with a postscript (1947), and Stokes, *op. cit.*, pp. 103-109.
[70] Stokes, *op. cit.*, p. 154.

form of cannibalism. Apparently he did not contemplate the predicament the human race would find itself in if at some future time man in his nobler and finer form should be able to detect a natural dignity and integrity in vegetables worthy of complete respect and sympathy. There can be no doubt that Shaw would have been equal to the task, and he did predict "the abandonment of food for sustaining life" and hoped that "'Some day ... we shall live on air.'"[71]

The extent to which Shaw found himself in political agreement with Shelley is apparent in his article *Shaming the Devil about Shelley:*

[Shelley was a] Republican, a Leveller, a Radical of the most extreme type.... He publicly ranged himself with demagogues and gaol-birds like Cobbett and Henry Hunt ... and not only advocated the "Plan of Radical Reform" which was afterwards embodied in the proposal of the Chartists, but denounced the rent-roll of the landed aristocracy as "the pension list", thereby classing himself as what we now call a Land Nationalizer. He echoed Cobbett's attacks on the National Debt and the Funding System in such a manner as to leave no reasonable doubt that if he had been born half a century later he would have been advocating Social-Democracy with a view to its development into the most democratic form of Communism practically attainable and maintainable.[72]

At a meeting honoring Shelley on August 4, 1892, Shaw made a speech in which he explained Shelley's opinions as he understood them and "declared that with every one of them he unreservedly agreed".[73]

Shaw's concurrence with Shelley was not limited to preaching political ideology. Like Shelley he lived according to his professed principles. He was involved in the riot which occurred on November 13, 1887, in Trafalgar Square when workers, victims of unemployment and depression, tried to hold a mass meeting in defiance of the police. As a result of this experience Shaw became convinced of the futility of violence as a means of securing

---

[71] Henderson, *op. cit.*, pp. 780-781.
[72] *Ibid.*, pp. 778-779, quoting George Bernard Shaw, "Shaming the Devil about Shelley", *The Albemarle*, II, No. 3 (September, 1892), 91-96.
[73] *Ibid.*, pp. 779-780.

reform.[74] He used his talents in an effort to persuade the government that Sir Roger Casement should be treated as a prisoner of war instead of tried for treason during World War I when Casement was caught in a futile effort to get German help in Ireland's struggle for independence.[75] His endorsement of Woodrow Wilson's plan for world peace through the establishment of a League of Nations and his rejection of arms races as a means of achieving national security are reminiscent of Shelley's views on standing armies as a cause of war and a world federation as a means of promoting peace. It seems clear that whatever Shaw derived from Shelley he put to work in his Fabian enterprises. More than any other individual he transmitted, and in some cases transmogrified, Shelley's political thought.

Since Shelleyan political thought may be easily traced into the twentieth century in England through Shaw and the Fabian Society, there remains the broader question of its impact, if any, outside of England. White in a note (*Shelley*, vol. II, pp. 639-641) summarizes the growth of Shelley's literary reputation in America and Europe (principally Germany, France, and Italy). But apparently there has been no extensive investigation of possible Shelleyan political influence upon Mohandas K. Gandhi and the great Indian struggle for independence which took place in the first half of this century. The subject is intriguing because of Gandhi's development of a technique of non-violent opposition which was similar in many respects to that advocated by Shelley as a means of securing reform.

Shelley's interest in Indian culture was lifelong, dating from his acquaintance with Dr. Lind at Eton. His poetry abounds with Indian imagery.[76] There is, however, no evidence to link Shelley directly with Indian affairs. In his time the British East India Company was gaining power and exploiting India, but the government did not take control until 1858. During the early part of the nineteenth century India and the Far East were being opened to commerce. An interest in oriental culture was devel-

[74] Hesketh Pearson, *G. B. S., A Full-Length Portrait*, chapter 11.
[75] Henderson, *op. cit.*, pp. 300-303.
[76] For an extended discussion of this topic, see Amiyakumar Sen, *Studies in Shelley*, chapter IV, "Shelley and Indian Thought", pp. 243-270.

oping in England and America. Thoreau's knowledge of the Hindu religion, particularly the *Bhagavad Gita*, influenced his essay "Civil Disobedience", which, in turn, influenced Gandhi. The Romantic poets often used oriental motifs. Shelley's setting for *The Revolt of Islam* is "Constantinople and modern Greece, but without much attempt at minute delineation of Mahometan manners" (letter of October 13, 1817, *Julian Works*, vol. IX, p. 251), and the opening scene of *Prometheus Unbound* finds Prometheus chained to a precipice in the Indian Caucasus. Though orientalism of this type was used primarily as ornamentation for works whose immediate background was European, there was an increasing awareness of the reality which lay concealed beneath the Romanticism of distant, relatively unknown lands. Explorers were returning from Asia and Africa not only with riches but with knowledge of the people. And some explorers understood the meaning of the changes which commerce was bringing to static or primitive societies and the significance of the spread of Shelleyan, or Shelley-like, ideas:

the explorer Henry M. Stanley warned an officer of the Shelley Society: "You are a funny people, you Shelleyites. You are playing – at a safe distance yourself, maybe, with fire. In spreading Shelley you are indirectly helping to stir up the great socialist question, the great question of the needs and wants and wishes of unhappy men; the one question which bids fair to swamp you all for a bit." [77]

The long Indian struggle for independence from British rule, which finally succeeded in 1947, would seem, on the surface, to be an unlikely place to look for Shelleyan political influence because of the religious character of its leader, Gandhi. But Gandhi was no ordinary religious leader. He formulated his own liturgy, as it were, and then used it as a means of effecting mass action. His development and application of the doctrine of nonviolent resistance, to which he gave the name Satyagraha, was the first large-scale demonstration that such a technique could be practical and effective. His course was not easy and not without fearful setbacks, but it succeeded. Since it closely parallels the "Quakerish and Socinian principles of politics" which Shelley

---

[77] N. I. White, *Shelley*, vol. II, p. 416.

hoped *An Address to the Irish People* would induce (*Julian Works*, vol. VIII, p. 254) – principles that he restated in other works – the problem of immediate interest is whether or not Gandhi read Shelley and derived to any extent the ideological foundation for his doctrine from him.

Gandhi was somewhat acquainted with Shelley's works, but the time during which he became acquainted has not been established. There is no mention of Shelley in his *An Autobiography*, but his familiarity with Shelley (at least partial familiarity) is revealed in his discussion with Christian leaders in December, 1938. Explaining how his program of Satyagraha might have been used by China as a means of countering Japanese aggression, he quotes from *The Mask of Anarchy*:

"If the Chinese had non-violence of my conception, there would be no use left for the latest machinery for destruction, which Japan possesses. The Chinese would say to Japan, 'Bring all your machinery. We present half of our population to you. But the remaining two hundred millions will not bend their knee to you.' If the Chinese did that, Japan would become China's slave." And in support of his argument he referred to Shelley's celebrated lines, "Ye are many – they are few."[78]

The line quoted is the last line of the poem. Another Gandhi biographer, Louis Fischer, in giving an account of what was apparently the same incident, says, "Gandhi once recited these verses of Shelley to a Christian gathering in India" and then quotes stanzas 79, 84, 85, 86, and 91 of *The Mask of Anarchy*, stanza 91 being the conclusion of the poem.[79] But this event showing Gandhi's knowledge and approval of Shelley's principle of non-violence as a means of reform occurred only ten years before his death and long after his technique of Satyagraha had been developed and successfully applied in South Africa and in India. The vital question concerns the time when he first learned of Shelley's views. If it could be determined that he read Shelley during his student days or when he was developing his doctrine of Satyagraha in South Africa between 1903 and 1914, the conclu-

[78] D. G. Tendulkar, *Mahatma*, vol. IV, p. 389.
[79] Louis Fischer, *The Life of Mahatma Gandhi*, pp. 118-119.

sion that Shelley exerted an influence upon his ideology would be inescapable.

Gandhi's schooling in England consisted largely of learning English manners and dress, though he underwent a period of intensive study of required subjects in preparation for the London Matriculation, and later the bar, examinations. The books he found of most interest were H. S. Salt's *Plea for Vegetarianism*, which made him a vegetarian by choice, though he was already one on religious grounds, the Bible (only the New Testament, especially the Sermon on the Mount), Carlyle's *Heroes and Hero-Worship*, and Mrs. Annie Besant's *How I Became a Theosophist*. His taste in reading ran to religious works, though he states that he had little time for reading anything other than textbooks in preparation for the bar examination.[80] There are other minor details of Gandhi's literary interests, but a thorough review of accounts of his period of schooling fails to disclose any evidence in support of a supposition that he read Shelley then.

Lacking autobiographical evidence as to the time when Gandhi first read Shelley, we have in *Indian Opinion*, which he published in South Africa from 1903 to 1914 during the campaign of non-violent resistance, a relatively complete record of his thinking during this period. It would seem reasonable to suppose that Shelley, or some of his works, would be cited at some place in this lengthy chronicle if Gandhi had read him either then or previously because Gandhi wrote extensively for the journal. He says,

So long as it was under my control, the changes in the journal were indicative of changes in my life. *Indian Opinion* in those days ... was a mirror of part of my life. Week after week I poured out my soul in its columns, and expounded the principles and practice of Satyagraha as I understood it. During ten years, that is, until 1914, excepting the intervals of my enforced rest in prison, there was hardly an issue of *Indian Opinion* without an article from me. I cannot recall a word in those articles set down without thought or deliberation, or a word of conscious exaggeration, or anything merely to please. Indeed the journal became for me a training in self-restraint, and for friends a medium through which to keep in touch with my thoughts.[81]

[80] Mohandas K. Gandhi, *An Autobiography*, p. 69.
[81] *Ibid.*, p. 286.

But there is no reference to Shelley in Gandhi's *Indian Opinion*. My search of the entire file of this publication for the years when Gandhi was publisher (1903-1914) failed to produce a single Shelley reference in any article written by Gandhi. It is likely that he did not make use of Shelley during his South African campaign because Shelley was not available to him. At the time Gandhi was working out a personal religious code which called for a life of strict simplicity devoid of all material possessions beyond necessities. He possessed few books and would not have considered a personal library a necessity.

The books which Gandhi received during his campaign of Satyagraha in South Africa were usually provided by his friend Henry S. L. Polak. It was Polak who gave him a copy of Ruskin's *Unto this Last* to read during a journey. Gandhi's account of his reading of this work reveals not only the effect that the book had upon him but also his limited reading habit:

This was the first book of Ruskin I had ever read. During the days of my education I had read practically nothing outside text-books, and after I launched into active life I had very little time for reading. I cannot therefore claim much book knowledge. However, I believe I have not lost much because of this enforced restraint. On the contrary, the limited reading may be said to have enabled me thoroughly to digest what I did read. Of these books, the one that brought about an instantaneous and practical transformation in my life was *Unto This Last*.[82]

Hence it may be seen that Gandhi was not widely read. He read intensively and reflectively the few books which caught his attention.

Judging from these facts concerning Gandhi's schooling and reading taste and habits and the fact that Shelley is not mentioned in any of the issues of *Indian Opinion*, we may safely conclude that he did not become acquainted with Shelley until sometime after 1914, the year which marked the end of his South African campaign.

Gandhi's summary of Ruskin's *Unto this Last* is contained in three principles:

[82] *Ibid.*, pp. 298-299.

1. That the good of the individual is contained in the good of all.
2. That a lawyer's work has the same value as the barber's inasmuch as all have the same right of earning their livelihood from their work.
3. That a life of labour, *i.e.*, the life of the tiller of the soil and the handicraftsman is the life worth living.[83]

The book gave Gandhi a new insight: he perceived that the second two principles were contained in the first, and he characteristically set about putting all of these principles into practice. The result was the establishment of the Phoenix Farm in South Africa with its ideals of agrarian life unencumbered by machinery and of service to humanity. This was the genesis of Satyagraha. Thus whatever literary influences touched Gandhi were always transformed by his experience and religious beliefs into specific practices, and we may conclude that any Shelleyan influence which was exerted upon him during this period came to him indirectly through Ruskin's *Unto this Last*.

Until, or unless, positive evidence is uncovered, not even satisfactory speculation as to the time when Gandhi first read Shelley can be made. All we can be reasonably certain of is that it occurred after 1914. He may have read him upon his return to India from victory in South Africa to lead the long and arduous struggle for Indian independence. It may have been during the Satyagraha campaigns in India or later, but whatever the time, it is obvious that he found in Shelley an eloquent statement of the principle he successfully employed in his revolutionary cause.

As was pointed out near the beginning of this study, when Shelley saw that his talents were not suited for the role of active reformer which he tried to play in Ireland, he decided,

I shall address myself no more to the illiterate. I will look to events in which it will be impossible that I can share, and make myself the cause of an effect which will take place ages after I have mouldered in the dust.[84]

Thereafter his primary concern was for writing poetry which would embody his ideas and vision, though he could not resist

---

[83] *Ibid.*, p. 299.
[84] Shelley to Godwin, March 18, 1812, *Julian Works*, vol. VIII, p. 301.

the temptation to support the cause of political reform in less exalted ways whenever an opportunity presented itself. The tracts are evidence of this. No political events have been traced directly and exclusively to specific Shelley proposals. But his writing, both the poetry and the prose, did reach and variously influence men of succeeding generations who played important roles in reform movements. It continues to do so. The kind of world-wide change which Shelley envisaged continues, with all its hazards, at an accelerated pace and in exactly the direction he pointed. It is doubtful that he would have wished for more political influence with the unknown generations to whom he addressed himself than he has obtained.

BIBLIOGRAPHY

I. PRIMARY SOURCES

Byron, George Gordon, Lord, *The Works of Lord Byron: Letters and Journals*, vol. IV (London, John Murray, Albemarle Street; New York, Charles Scribner's Sons, 1900).

Gandhi, Mohandas Karamchand, *An Autobiography or the Story of My Experiments with Truth*. Translated from the original in Gujarati by Mahadev Desai (Ahmedabad, Navajivan Press, 1940).

Godwin, William, *Enquiry Concerning Political Justice*, 2 vols. (London, J. Watson, 1842).

Macaulay, Thomas B., *Miscellaneous Works of Lord Macaulay*. Edited by his sister Lady Trevelyan, 5 vols. (New York, Harper & Brothers, Publishers, 1880).

Paine, Thomas, *Basic Writings of Thomas Paine (Common Sense, Rights of Man, Age of Reason)* (New York, Willey Book Company, 1942).

Ruskin, John, *The Works of John Ruskin*. Edited by E. T. Cook and Alexander Wedderburn, 39 vols. (New York, Longmans, Green, and Co., 1903-1912).

Shaw, George Bernard, *Back to Methuselah*. Revised Edition with a Postscript. The World's Classics Galaxy Edition, No. 1 (London, Oxford University Press, 1947).

——, *Prefaces* (London, Constable & Company Ltd., 1934).

Shelley, Percy Bysshe, *The Complete Works of Percy Bysshe Shelley*. Edited by Roger Ingpen and Walter E. Peck. Julian Editions, 10 vols. (New York, Charles Scribner's Sons, 1926-1930).

——, *The Complete Poetical Works of Percy Bysshe Shelley*. Edited by Thomas Hutchinson (New York, Oxford University Press, 1933).

——, *The Complete Poetical Works of Percy Bysshe Shelley*. Student's Cambridge Edition (New York, Houghton Mifflin Company, 1901).

——, *Shelley's Prose*. Edited by David Lee Clark (Albuquerque, The University of New Mexico Press, 1954).

Swinburne, Algernon Charles, *The Complete Works of Algernon Charles Swinburne*. Edited by Sir Edmund Gosse and Thomas James Wise. Bonchurch Edition, 20 vols. (London, William Heinemann Ltd., 1925-1927).

II. SECONDARY SOURCES

Baker, Carlos, *Shelley's Major Poetry: The Fabric of a Vision* (Princeton, New Jersey, Princeton University Press, 1948).
Cameron, Kenneth Neill, "The Political Symbolism of *Prometheus Unbound*". *PMLA (Publications of the Modern Language Association of America)*, vol. LVIII (September, 1943), pp. 728-753.
——, *The Young Shelley* (New York, The Macmillan Company, 1950).
Cook, E. T., *The Life of John Ruskin*, 2 vols. (New York, The Macmillan Company, 1911).
DeVane, William C. (ed.), *The Shorter Poems of Robert Browning*. Edited with an introduction by William C. DeVane (New York, Appleton-Century-Crofts, Inc., 1934).
Dowden, Edward, *Transcripts and Studies*. Second Edition (London, Kegan Paul, Trench, Trubner & Co., Ltd., 1896).
Fain, John Tyree, *Ruskin and the Economists* (Nashville, Vanderbilt University Press, 1956).
Fischer, Louis, *The Life of Mahatma Gandhi* (New York, Harper and Brothers, 1950).
Gosse, Edmund, *The Life of Algernon Charles Swinburne* (London, Macmillan and Co., Limited, 1917).
Grabo, Carl, *The Magic Plant* (Chapel Hill, The University of North Carolina Press, 1936).
Henderson, Archibald, *George Bernard Shaw: Man of the Century* (New York, Appleton-Century-Crofts, Inc., 1956).
Hogg, Thomas Jefferson, *The Life of Percy Bysshe Shelley* (London, George Routledge & Sons Limited, 1906).
Leith, Mrs. Disney, *Algernon Charles Swinburne* (New York, G. P. Putnam's Sons, 1917).
Medwin, Thomas, *The Life of Percy Bysshe Shelley*. Edited by H. Buxton Forman. A new edition printed from a copy copiously amended and extended by the author and left unpublished at his death with an introduction and commentary by H. Buxton Forman (London, Oxford University Press, 1913).
Miller, Betty, *Robert Browning: A Portrait* (London, John Murray, 1952).
Norman, Sylva, *Flight of the Skylark* (London, Max Reinhardt Ltd., 1954).
Pearson, Hesketh, *G. B. S., A Full-Length Portrait* (Garden City, N.Y., Garden City Publishing Co., Inc., 1946).
Sen, Amiyakumar, *Studies in Shelley* (Published by the University of Calcutta, 1936).
Shaw, George Bernard, "Shaming the Devil about Shelley", *The Albemarle*, vol. II, no. 3 (September, 1892), pp. 91-96.
The Shelley Society's Papers, vol. I, Parts I and II, *The Shelley Society's Publications*, First Series, No. 1 (London, Published for the Shelley Society by Reeves and Turner, 1888).
Stokes, Elmore Ewing, Jr., *Shelley and Bernard Shaw: A Study in Late Nineteenth Century Socialism*. A thesis presented to the faculty of the graduate school of the University of Texas in partial fulfillment of

the requirements for the degree of master of arts (Austin, Texas, May, 1948).

Tendulkar, D. G., *Mahatma: Life of Mohandas Karamchand Gandhi*, 8 vols. (Bombay, The Times of India Press, 1951-1954).

[Tennyson, Hallam], *Alfred Lord Tennyson*. A memoir by his son, 2 vols. (New York, The Macmillan Company, 1897).

Thomas, Edward, *Algernon Charles Swinburne* (New York, Mitchell Kennerley, 1912).

White, Newman Ivey, "Literature and the Law of Libel: Shelley and the Radicals of 1840-1842", *Studies in Philology*, vol. XXII (January, 1925), pp. 34-47.

——, "Shelley and the Active Radicals of the Early Nineteenth Century", *South Atlantic Quarterly*, vol. XXIX (July, 1930), pp. 248-261.

——, *Shelley*, 2 vols. (New York, Alfred A. Knopf, 1947).

STUDIES IN ENGLISH LITERATURE

1. WILLIAM H. MATCHETT: *The Phoenix and the Turtle: Shakespeare's Poem and Chester's Loues Martyr.* 1965. 213 pp. Cloth. Gld. 26.—

5. DOROTHY SCHUCHMAN MCCOY: *Tradition and Convention: A Study of Periphrasis in English Pastoral Poetry from 1556-1715.* 1965. 289 pp. Gld. 30.—

6. TED E. BOYLE: *Symbol and Meaning in the Fiction of Joseph Conrad.* 1965. 245 pp. Gld. 24.—

8. GERARD ANTHONY PILECKI: *Shaw's "Geneva": A Critical Study of the Evolution of the Text in Relation to Shaw's Political Thought and Dramatic Practice.* 1965. 189 pp. Gld. 20.—

9. BLAZE ODELL BONAZZA: *Shakespeare's Early Comedies: A Structural Analysis.* 1966. 125 pp. Cloth. Gld. 18.—

10. THOMAS KRANIDAS: *The Fierce Equation: A Study of Milton's Decorum.* 1965. 165 pp. Cloth. Gld. 21.—

11. KENNETH HUGH BYRON: *The Pessimism of James Thomson (B.V.) in Relation to his Times.* 1965. 174 pp. Cloth. Gld. 20.—

12. ROLAND A. DUERKSEN: *Shelleyan Ideas in Victorian Literature.* 1966. 208 pp. Cloth. Gld. 24.—

13. EARL J. SCHULZE: *Shelley's Theory of Poetry: A Reappraisal.* 1966. 237 pp. Gld. 29.—

14. CHARLOTTE BRADFORD HUGHES: *John Crowne's "Sir Courtly Nice": A Critical Edition.* 1966. 183 pp. Gld. 23.—

16. BARBARA BARTHOLOMEW: *Fortuna and Natura: A Reading of Three Chaucer Narratives.* 1966. 112 pp. Cloth. Gld. 17.—

17. GEORG B. FERGUSON: *John Fletcher: The Woman's Prize or The Tamer Tamed. A Critical Edition.* 1966. 223 pp. Cloth. Gld. 24.—

18. EDWARD VASTA: *The Spiritual Basis of "Piers Plowman".* 1965. 143 pp. Cloth. Gld. 18.—

19. WILLIAM B. TOOLE: *Shakespeare's Problem Plays: Studies in Form and Meaning.* 1966. 242 pp. Cloth. Gld. 28.—

20. LOUISE BAUGHMAN MURDY: *Sound and Meaning in Dylan Thomas's Poetry*. 1966. 172 pp., 11 spectograms. Gld. 21.—

21. BEN H. SMITH JR.: *Traditional Imagery of Charity in "Piers Plowman"*. 1966. 106 pp. Gld. 14.—

22. OVERTON P. JAMES: *The Relation of Tristram Shandy to the Life of Sterne*. 1966. 174 pp. Gld. 21.—

23. LOUIS TONKO MILIC: *A Quantitative Approach to the Style of Jonathan Swift*. 1967. 317 pp., 56 tables, 15 figs., folding key. Gld. 34.—

25. WILLIAM M. WIJNKOOP: *Three Children of the Universe: Emerson's View of Shakespeare, Bacon, and Milton*. 1966. 199 pp., portrait. Cloth. Gld. 22.—

28. SOPHIA BLAYDES: *Christopher Smart as a Poet of His Time: A Re-Appraisal*. 1966. 182 pp. Gld. 24.—

29. ROBERT R. HODGES: *The Dual Heritage of Joseph Conrad*. 1967. 229 pp. Gld. 27.—

30. GEORGE R. LEVINE: *Henry Fielding and the Dry Mock: A Study of the Techniques of Irony in His Early Works*. 1967. 160 pp. Gld. 20.—

31. ERIC LAGUARDIA: *Nature Redeemed: The Imitation of Order in Three Renaissance Poems*. 1966. 180 pp. Gld. 20.—

34. ROBERT DONALD SPECTOR: *English Literary Periodicals and the Climate of Opinion during the Seven Year's War*. 1966. 408 pp. Gld. 40.—

MOUTON • PUBLISHERS • THE HAGUE

10-21-69